CIVIL

A PRACTICAL GUIDE

Cavendish
Publishing
Limited

CIVIL ADVOCACY

A PRACTICAL GUIDE

JACQUI GILLIATT, Barrister, CHARLES BOURNE, Barrister and PRASHANT POPAT, Barrister

First published in Great Britain 1997 by Cavendish Publishing Limited, The Glass House, Wharton Street, London WC1X 9PX.

Telephone: 0171-278 8000 Facsimile: 0171-278 8080

Bourne, Charles

Civil Advocacy: A Practical Guide

I. Title II. Popat, Prashant

344.2071

ISBN 1 874241 12 0

Printed and bound in Great Britain by
Biddles Ltd, Guildford and King's Lynn

Preface

> Politics is perhaps the only profession for which no preparation is thought necessary. *

The same is not true of advocacy. Unfortunately, the realities of legal aid cuts, impoverished clients who cannot put solicitors in funds until the last moment and the hazards of listing mean that advocates often do not have the luxury of time to prepare. This is a particular problem for the inexperienced advocate, but even the old hand can be taken by surprise when asked to take over a colleague's case at the last moment. If there is time, use it. This book is no substitute for legal textbooks. But if there is little time available, then we hope that this book will provide a coping mechanism. We also hope it will show you how to use the time that you have efficiently and effectively, so that when you do have to jump into action you will at least know where the hurdles are.

If you are intending to make advocacy a substantial part of your career, it is likely that you will undergo a lengthy period of training. Use that time to identify the sorts of cases you are most likely to meet in your early years and try to attend the courts and tribunals in which you are likely to be appearing. Your familiarity with the procedures of the European Court of Human Rights will not be much help in the Inner London Family Proceedings Court. Try and develop a pack of key materials for the most common applications: the key cases, extracts from statutes and regulations, etc. Reference is made to suitable materials throughout this book. Make sure you know which are the most useful books to take to court: see the suggestions we make in each chapter of this book.

This book is deliberately aimed at all advocates and not just barristers, but, where stated, some comments only apply to counsel and many of the references in this book assume that someone other than the advocate has put the papers together.

We have concentrated in the main on county court procedures, on the basis that the inexperienced advocate is more likely to be appearing in a county court. However, significant differences in High Court procedure are noted.

We have included references to Lord Woolf's report on 'Access to Justice', the Woolf Report, July 1996, HMSO, where appropriate, although there is, as yet, no information about the timetable for implementation.

The law is stated as at 30 September 1996.

Jacqui Gilliatt, Charles Bourne, Prashant Popat
September 1996

*Stevenson, RL, *Familiar Studies of Men and Books*, 1882, 'Yoshida-Torajiro'.

Acknowledgments

We are very grateful to the following members of the Bar for their invaluable assistance:

Oliver Campbell

Richard Colbey

Dorian Drew

Gwynneth Knowles

Mary Lazarus

Stephen Monkcom

Wendy Outhwaite

Geraint Webb

Isabella Zornoza

We are also very grateful to the following:

Barry Dainton

Louise Rush

Hugh Seckleman

Contents

Table of Cases

Table of Statutes

Table of Rules

County Court Rules

Supreme Court Rules

Table of Statutory Instruments

Table of Practice Directions and Notes

1 : Travelling and arriving

The destination

First check the brief. Look also for any document from the court such as a summons or notice of hearing. They do not always correspond. Avoid common mistakes like confusing Brentwood with Brentford. Be particularly careful about courts with overspill locations or two buildings and with the Inner London Family Proceedings Court which sits all over London from Balham to Marylebone. Keep an eye on court notice boards which will tell you of any impending moves.

Check the listed time and check also to see what time you or the client have been asked to arrive.

County courts, Crown Courts and magistrates' courts on the south-eastern and western circuits are listed in *The Court Guide* by Andrew Goodman (Blackstone Press), an annual publication which gives the address, phone number, details of facilities, opening times and directions for those travelling by public transport or car. For all other locations of these courts and for High Court Registries, see *Shaw's Directory of Courts*. Unfortunately, this does not give directions. County court addresses are also given at the back of the *Green Book*. Check with colleagues, ring the court, or solicitors if local.

How to get there

In general, trains are safer than cars: when they go wrong they are easier to abandon, you do not need to park them, and they usually know where they are going. And, of course, the journey gives you time to read through the case papers (again).

NOTES:

Always check train times from an up-to-date British Rail ABC Guide. If it is your first time to a particular court (and even if it is not), it is a good rule to take the train before the one you think you need, where practicable. If you can afford it, it also makes sense to take a taxi until you know your way around. Next time it is up to you!

Arrive in plenty of time to find your way around the court building and to get through the checklist in the next section. Allow at least 30 minutes before the hearing.

On arrival

On arrival, this basic approach, give or take, is recommended to start you off.

Look at the list. Note the name of the judge or other presiding officer, the court number and the number or position in the list. See whether you are in open court or chambers. Make a mental note of the names of cases before and after you (you will hear them being called out).

Go to the advocates' room if there is one. You may need a security code to get in, which you will normally get from the usher or the security guard. Robe, if necessary, and collect together what you need, ie case papers and books. Leave the rest of your possessions except valuables. There is a traditional view that advocates are not expected to enter the court carrying briefcases, but this is not always practical. Ask the court staff if there is anywhere else where you can leave your belongings (sometimes you can park them at the back of the court) but be careful not to set off a security alert.

Locate the usher (or clerk, etc). Smile! Say who you are and point out which case you are in. The usher may take your name, or send you away, or ask you to fill in a slip.

NOTES:

Ask whether the other side have arrived (note the name of their advocate), and whether your client/witnesses are there yet.

Ask whether the list is being taken in its written order. If you have a time problem, say so. If you are going to be very quick, say so, you may get on sooner. Do not abuse this. Court staff and other advocates get very annoyed about over-optimistic time estimates and advocates who always expect special treatment.

Tell the usher where you will be, eg in a consultation room, in case anything happens.

Locate your client and introduce yourself, if necessary. Remember the need to help client/witnesses relax and not worry about the ordeal ahead. Make sure that the client knows what is going to happen in the court room, who will be present, and how they should address the court. If, as is often the case, it looks as if you will all be there for a long time, explain this and find out whether this causes any problems for the client such as child minding/collecting, signing on for benefit, etc and what can be done about it.

Make contact with your opponent. Think carefully about what you need to discuss, eg evidence you propose to adduce to which he or she may object, the scope of the dispute, whether a chronology is agreed, whether there are any areas of agreement such as quantum. What else you say to your opponent about your case is difficult to advise on in the abstract. In some situations, for example, you might want to float an idea for compromise with your opponent before taking instructions from your client. You must make it clear whether or not you are speaking with instructions. It may be useful to talk through the basis on which each side is putting their case in general terms so that you know in what order to take things when before the court. Whilst you should avoid the temptation to try to persuade your opponent of the superiority of your case (and do not allow them to bully you either), it is sometimes helpful to suggest points which could assist them in persuading their client to accept a settlement. On other occasions, you may wish to be more circumspect. A great deal may depend on how well you know your opponent and the tribunal. There is a difficult balance to be struck between the modern tendency towards openness and the need to be discreet whilst putting forward the strongest possible case on behalf of your client. Remember that provided you are not making admissions (and you should only make them with the permission of your client), your discussions outside court are confidential and whatever your opponent may have gleaned about your personal confidence in your own case cannot be passed on and should not be revealed by your behaviour in the courtroom.

It is increasingly common to encounter litigants-in-person as opponents and special care is needed. Try and assess their mood, which will often be very nervous. Explain first that they do not have to speak to you if they do not want to, but, if appropriate, that there are one or two things which you need to tell them about or documents you need to show them. Emphasise that you are acting for the other side so that you cannot give them legal advice but that you can tell them about procedure in court if there is anything they want to know, such as what to call the judge, and who will be in the courtroom. It may be helpful to find out whether they have received any legal advice about the case before coming to court and whether they intend to be legally represented in future. After these preliminaries you should be able to judge whether you can go further or whether it would be

NOTES:

better to leave matters to the court. Remember that you can always ask the judge to explain things to the litigant or to confirm any points that you have made (such as the effect of giving undertakings).

Keep the usher informed of progress; whether you are reaching or have reached an agreement or whether you need extra time to talk. Try and give an accurate estimate of how long your case is going to take once you are ready to go in.

Other practicalities

You might need to carry with you:

- change for phone, tickets, parking meters, coffee machines;
- mobile phone and/or a BT charge card;
- spare supplies of notebooks, collar studs, hairgrips, tights;
- tissues;
- calculator;
- highlighter pen;
- post-it notes for flagging pages and documents.

What if ...?

You oversleep, get held up or go to the wrong court?

If possible, telephone the court and explain, quoting the case number and saying how long you are likely to be; failing that, telephone your clerk/office and ask them to inform the court. What happens then will depend on how late you are. If you can arrive well within office hours, the case is likely to be held up until you arrive. On arrival, make yourself known. Offer fulsome apologies to your client, your opponent, and, when you go into the court, the judge. On

Notes:

the other hand, if you are so late that the case cannot be heard that day, it will be adjourned. Maintain contact with the court until the position is clear; there may be no point in your going to court at all.

You arrive at court but your case is not on any list?

Check with the usher as to what is on their list as it is often different from the one pinned up on the board or left with security. If this is fruitless, ask the usher where to go next: this will usually be the court office or enquiry point. Make sure you have the case number with you. If it is a court error, it may be possible to seek compensation from the Lord Chancellor's Department. If it is someone else's fault, you may wish to consider whether to charge for your wasted time.

You do not have your robes when you should?

Try to borrow some, for example, from someone whose case has just finished. If this is not possible, speak to the usher or clerk who may be able to give you a clue as to the judge's likely reaction or may be prepared to ask the judge if he or she will hear you regardless. In court, when you are called upon, stand up and immediately apologise for not being robed (if your opponent would normally open, ask if you can mention it first). Explain briefly why and ask the judge if, in the circumstances, he or she will hear you notwithstanding. If the answer is yes, carry on as normal. Again, in the unlikely event that the answer is no, immediately ask:

> *In the circumstances, would your Honour consent to an adjournment until [such time as you can obtain robes/if no possibility of obtaining robes, to the first open date].*

NOTES:

In the unlikely event of the judge refusing to hear you even to that extent, ask your opponent to request the adjournment for you.

If you are robed unnecessarily, simply remove your wig (where applicable) and gown in court. The judge will not mind you wearing neckbands.

The court refuses to hear you?

For example, you are a trainee solicitor in a county court, and the judge believes someone more experienced should have attended. The best you can do is ask for an adjournment to the first open date. If the judge will not hear you, even for that purpose, again, ask your opponent to assist. If you have no opponent, the judge will simply decide what to do: usually an adjournment.

A vital witness or your client does not turn up?

Check, via your office or those instructing you, that the person has been correctly informed of the hearing. Try to have them telephoned. See whether any message has been sent to the court: they may have gone to the wrong building. In a large court building have a good look around or ask for them to be paged. If it is possible to get the person to court fairly quickly, go into court when your case is called, explain and ask for a short adjournment. It is courteous to explain the situation to your opponent beforehand. If there is no prospect of the missing person coming in time for the hearing, ask for an adjournment to the first open date (preferably having checked that the missing person will have no further availability problem). If it is a witness who is missing, check that your client understands the costs implications of this; they might prefer to go ahead.

NOTES:

You are the instructing solicitor and counsel has not arrived?

If you know that counsel is going to attend, but has been delayed, ask the court (either via the usher or in court) for an adjournment until they arrive, explaining, if you can, what the problem is. If you find out that counsel is not coming or is not likely to get there at a reasonable time, you will have to consider whether you are in a position to conduct the hearing yourself, taking your client's instructions. If you cannot take over, you will have to ask for an adjournment. You will no doubt wish to consider who should be responsible for any costs incurred after the hearing!

The instructing solicitor has not arrived?

Strictly speaking, when counsel has been briefed the instructing solicitor should attend unless it has been specifically agreed otherwise. First, find out whether the solicitor is expected to attend. If not, then you can go ahead, unless you feel you really need to have them there for some reason. If you discover they are expected then you should ask the court to delay the hearing until they arrive; they are your clients as much as the lay client and you should not proceed without their instructions. If the court is keen to go ahead before they arrive, you will have to use your common sense and judgment, depending on the facts of the case, how fully briefed you are, how well you know the solicitor and so on. In many cases, the solicitor is more likely to want to avoid wasting costs and will prefer that you go ahead. You may be able to get authority for this from someone else in the firm by telephone.

The other side doesn't turn up?

There may be excellent reasons for this. You have no duty to make enquiries, unless you are asked to do so by the court.

NOTES:

However, check who was supposed to serve them with notice; this can be particularly confusing in family proceedings. The court will probably want to know about relevant correspondence and telephone conversations with the other side. Otherwise, you are perfectly entitled to proceed with your application (or ask for the other side's application to be dismissed) in the absence of opposition. Needless to say, you are likely to win (although, if you were expecting them to turn up, the court may very well give them the benefit of the doubt). However, beware any procedural shortcomings in the preparation of your case. Without anyone to take issue, the court may take it upon itself to police such points with vigilance. Be prepared to explain why such a course will not result in injustice. Bear in mind the provisions of CCR Order 37 r (2) (and RSC Order 32 rr 5 and 6) which allow the court to set aside a judgment given in the absence of a party. You should ensure that your client is aware that it is not necessarily the end of the matter.

NOTES:

2 : Courtroom basics

Inside the courtroom

Courtrooms are not as intimidating and formal as they once were. However, there are a few golden rules which, if you observe them, should mean that you do not upset your tribunal before you even open your mouth!

- On entering or leaving any court sitting in open court (but not, in general, tribunals), bow to whomever is presiding over the court. If the court has a 'bar' in front of which only lawyers go, bow on entering this area. Otherwise bow near the door of the court, at a point where you are visible to the judge. It need not be a deep bow and tends to become merely a nod. However, it is polite to make it a clear gesture from a stationary position, as opposed to letting it simply merge into your progress to or from the door.
- Once in court, try to sit in the right place. In the High Court and Crown Court (and any higher courts), the front main bench, with lecterns, is reserved for QCs (the very front bench, in front of which there is no table, may be occupied by solicitors). Junior counsel should not sit here, even in a crowded court, unless invited by the judge. The next row is for junior counsel. The row after that is for solicitors. These rules are often applied quite strictly.

  In a county court or magistrates' court, the front bench is for counsel, and the second is for solicitors and parties. The actual practice in these courts is much more flexible, especially when they are crowded. Often advocates move to the front row when the time comes for them to address the court.

Notes:

In general, in civil cases (open court and chambers), the plaintiff sits on the judge's right (your left). In practice, it may depend on the layout of the court. An usher may tell you where to go, or there may be witness boxes marked 'Plaintiff' and 'Defendant' in which case you should sit nearer the applicable one.

- It is quite all right to move around the courtroom and communicate in whispers with other people (but try not to walk between the judge and the advocates' bench). It is often necessary to keep the usher or court clerk updated about developments which may affect the hearing of your case, eg by passing a note. It is not unusual for one advocate to ask to consult a book which another has with him or her. During the hearing of your case, you are free to communicate *sotto voce* with your opponent, to prompt him as to, say, a name which he is struggling to remember, or to correct a fundamental error which he makes in opening and which might mislead a judge.

  NB: There is one important exception to the principle that you may move around and talk in court. Whenever someone is taking an oath, you should freeze, and motion to your client to stop talking.

Ideally, a judge should not be left alone in open court. The last advocate in court should either wait for the judge to leave or ask permission to withdraw. In theory, the same applies in magistrates' courts, though many magistrates will not insist on it.

Advocacy

It has been said that the medium is the message. This may seem to conflict with the principle that the point of any court hearing is to ensure that justice is done and that it is seen to

NOTES:

be done. However, the job of the advocate is to persuade the tribunal to see things from their client's point of view. It is hoped that some of what follows will help you to do that or at the very least prevent you from obscuring your message.

Personal presentation

- Even if you do not feel confident, act as if you are – you may be surprised how much better this will make you feel.
- Don't forget that your opponent will not necessarily be as aware of the shortcomings in your case as you are.
- However, think through the opposing arguments so that you can deal with them.
- Identify any irritating mannerisms (for example, moving about, fiddling with jewellery), you might have and make an effort to eliminate them – ask friends and colleagues or watch other people and consider whether you do anything similar.
- Watch the judge's pen as you are speaking and make sure he or she has time to note down what you are saying.
- Always be polite: even if you think the judge is completely wrong, it should never show – apologise, say please, suggest there are other matters which should be taken into account, whatever it takes.
- Do not express your personal opinions unless specifically invited to do so: do not say 'I think' or 'in my opinion'. You must 'submit' or 'contend' or say 'it was the opinion of the court in that case'. As John Mortimer put it: 'Detachment is all: what is to be aimed at is the state of lucid indifference' (*Clinging to the Wreckage*, 1983, Penguin).

NOTES:

- Be very careful with your use of the expression 'my instructions are' or 'I am instructed'. If, for example, it is said to contrast your instructions with that of your opponent ('My opponent's case is that there was no damage to the car after the collision, whereas my instructions are that the front bumper was dented and hanging down'), it may be acceptable. However, it can distance you from your client in a way which suggests you do not believe them.
- Do not make excuses for defects in your case; apologise and ask the court to waive any defect if it has the power to do so pointing out, if you can, why the other side is not prejudiced. For example, if the pleadings are incomplete but the basis of the case is clear from the correspondence, this does not excuse the defect in the pleadings, but it might be good enough to persuade the court to exercise a discretion.
- Check whether you need to be robed (set out in the following chapters). Some judges still expect robes to be carried everywhere just in case but, fortunately, they are rare. In general, robes are not required in the magistrates' courts, tribunals or at hearings in chambers, however, robes are required at all other open court hearings.
- Check how you should address the court (see Table opposite).

NOTES:

Modes of address: summary

Officer	*Direct*	*Indirect*
High Court judges, any other judge in High Court, Court of Appeal or House of Lords, Circuit judges in the Old Bailey	My Lord/Lady	Your Lordship/ Ladyship
Circuit judges in other courts, Recorders in Crown/ county court	Your Honour	Your Honour
Masters	Master	You
District judges, Magistrates, Tribunal Chairpersons, Coroners ...	Sir/Madam	You (and your colleagues)
Justices' clerks	Sir/Madam	Your learned clerk, You

The facts of the case

Make a list of the basic facts: names, dates, places and statements/affidavits. If possible, in the time, type out a chronology, cross reference to documents and so on. It is also increasingly common for courts to expect written skeletons, even in relatively simple cases. Use schedules to deal with complex figures. Chronologies should be as neutral as possible and state facts not make comments. Try and get your opponent's agreement to the contents. Even if it is not completely agreed, it may be useful to hand it to the judge and ask him or her to note any disputed areas.

NOTES:

The judge/tribunal

Know your judge: ask colleagues and others at court what the judge is like if you are in front of someone you do not know. Some judges are much more technically minded than others and will spot procedural defects immediately. It is better to deal with these straightaway, apologise and ask the court to overlook them. Many defects can be got round. We will deal with this in more detail in later chapters.

Find out how much the judge knows about the case and/or area of law before you begin speaking.

If you think the judge is familiar with the law, for example, the main case on summary judgments or ouster injunctions, it will usually be sufficient to refer to the main phrase used in the case, eg 'fair probability of a defence' or 'draconian order', rather than citing the case reference and full facts. You must be prepared to do this, if asked. A Recorder, for example, may not have seen a perfectly ordinary running down action for some time.

If there is time before your case is called on and the court is in open session, spend a few minutes watching the tribunal: this may alert you to any peculiar local practices or foibles of the tribunal. It may also remind you of a vital question to check with your client.

The case papers

Always check the papers in your instructions as soon as you get them and ask for anything that is missing or check that it will be available at court and/or has been filed with the court.

Check for obvious procedural defects. A simple example is provided by affidavits: does it have the right information in

NOTES:

the top right-hand corner? If it is in support of an *ex parte* application, does it explain that an order is needed urgently? If it is an affidavit of service, does it say that it was sworn by someone over the age of 16, does it say how they recognised the person they served and does it exhibit something which tells the party served when they are expected to attend court?

Check whether the judge has the file! It is quite common for the judge to have nothing at all or to have all the old papers but nothing relating to your particular application. Check that he or she has the key statements or affidavits. Affidavits of service have a particular habit of going missing as they tend to be filed very shortly before the hearing.

Check whether there is any new material to be filed, in particular, affidavits (especially affidavits of service).

Get hold of any forms you need from the office before going into court, eg undertakings forms, order forms, etc.

Witnesses

When thinking about questions to put to witnesses, first remember to identify the answer you want to obtain.

Check whether a question is leading, ie a question which suggests a particular answer. These are impermissible with your own witnesses.

Identify areas to explore with witnesses which are not covered by your instructions or statements and try and get answers before you go into court.

Check which witnesses you can speak to. For barristers, this point is dealt with in the Code of Conduct at paragraph 607.

NOTES:

In a case where witness statements have been filed, try to think of a few introductory questions so that the witness is not thrown in 'cold' to the mercy of your opponent's cross-examination. Even in fairly simple cases, a limited examination-in-chief will usually be allowed by the judge. Rules recommended by the Woolf Report will specifically allow the court to accept amplification of witness statements. The report also discourages the inclusion in witness statements of comments on documents so that questions about documents may have to form part of the examination-in-chief.

Check whether sufficient time has been allowed for any pre-trial conference.

Check that the witness has read over his own statement and any other relevant material before he or she goes into court and specifically whether there are any inaccuracies.

Check whether the witness has any court experience and, if relevant, any criminal convictions.

Do not thank witnesses for answers given in court. This is an example of an irritating mannerism and wastes time. Also, avoid repeating the last few words of an answer unless you can use them as part of the next question.

Do not comment on the witness's answers; turn the comment into a question.

Do not ask the witness to speculate, eg 'Why do you think he or she did that?' (unless you know the witness formed a significant opinion from what he or she saw or heard). If necessary, ask whether the other person gave any explanation for their actions or statements.

NOTES:

Purpose of hearing

It might seem too obvious for words but think about it. It is surprising how often this is not clear from the instructions, particularly if the instructions have come to you from a colleague, with little or no update. Clients do not always want what you expect them to want.

Make sure you know where the court gets the power to do whatever you or the other side is asking them to do.

Consider whether the hearing can be effective.

If you do not think it can, consider what can be salvaged. Remember that even if a hearing is non-effective there may be directions which will progress matters and you may have to deal with costs. With the implementation of the Woolf Report, the court is going to be increasingly demanding about keeping to timetables and advocates will have to work harder to persuade them of the necessity of adjournments especially if they are to avoid sanctions being imposed.

Try and anticipate typical problems, eg requests for adjournments, amendments and so on.

Check the appeal provisions or at least where they are so that you know how long you have got to think about appealing and whether you need leave.

What if ... ?

On arrival at court you realise that there is a procedural flaw in your case?

In the county court, CCR Order 37 r 5 allows the court to treat any non-compliance with the rules as irregularities and gives the court wide powers to deal with such problems.

NOTES:

This even applies to proceedings started in the wrong way (see CCR Order 3 r 4 and RSC Order 2 r 1(3)). If the other side is not prejudiced, the court may be prepared to ignore the problem, eg by treating an application said to be under one rule as an application under a different rule. It may be possible to amend the pleadings (see CCR Order 15 and RSC Order 20) and dispense with re-service. If a document has not been filed or proceedings have not been issued, the court may be willing to accept an undertaking to make good the deficiency within a short time frame. You must try your best to avoid an adjournment which will cost the client money, but sometimes it will be inevitable.

If you do not have a copy of the *Green Book* with you to check the rules, you may be able to borrow one from someone else at court. Some courts have a library facility.

There are relatively few situations when a case is so fundamentally flawed that you cannot go on. This might happen when there was no cause of action when the proceedings were issued or if the wrong form is used to start possession proceedings (the form for possession contains certain vital information which must be brought to the attention of the defendant). Depending on the circumstances, you may simply have to allow the case to be dismissed or ask the court to non-suit the plaintiff under CCR Order 21 (there is no High Court equivalent). This may be better than having the claim dismissed since it allows the plaintiff to start the proceedings again, hopefully taking steps to make sure that the same mistake is not made again.

Don't forget that you may be able to negotiate a settlement. Even if the other side has spotted the problem, if they know that you will only re-issue, they might still be prepared to compromise.

NOTES:

The judge has no papers?

If the file cannot be found at all, you will have to see whether between you and your opponent you can come up with enough spare copies for the judge. Most courts have photocopying facilities but these are prohibitively expensive (£1 a page) so you may be better off in a local copy shop if there is one.

The other side has not been served?

If this is the responsibility of your team, you may have to explain firstly, what went wrong with service and secondly, why the court was not notified and the hearing vacated. You will probably have to ask for an adjournment or make an application for substituted service (CCR Order 7 r 8 and RSC Order 65 r 4).

NOTES:

3 : Interlocutory applications

An application made in the period after the issue of proceedings but before the final hearing is called an interlocutory application (such applications can be made before proceedings are begun in exceptional circumstances). Applications may be made *ex parte*, where the other party has not been notified, or *inter partes*, where notice has been given. Generally, an *ex parte* application can only be made where it is impossible to find and serve the other party or it is urgent or there is some legitimate reason for keeping the other party in the dark. Normally, a 'liberty to apply' is implicit in any interlocutory order so that the other party can ask for an early hearing *inter partes*. The applicant must serve the order on the other party immediately, along with any affidavit evidence filed in support of the application.

The main rules governing interlocutory applications are CCR Order 13 and RSC Orders 25 and 32 but other rules will be relevant depending on the order required, for example, CCR Order 9 r 14 for summary judgment. The *Green Book* and *White Book* notes are very thorough and refer to relevant cases. Most interlocutory applications require an affidavit in support and, although the court has the power to allow oral evidence (CCR Order 20 rr 5 and 9, RSC Order 38 r 2(3)), it will usually proceed on the basis of written evidence alone. Affidavits are not always required, for example, in support of fairly straightforward applications for directions.

The rule governing the form of affidavits is CCR Order 20 r 10 (RSC Order 41) and an affidavit which does not comply with the procedural requirements may be rejected (*Practice Note* [1983] 1 WLR 922). On *ex parte* applications, the affidavit must make full and frank disclosure of all matters

NOTES:

relevant to the case (even those which go against the applicant) and, if the application is for an *ex parte* injunction, the affidavit must explain why it is made *ex parte* (CCR Order 13 r 6; *RSC Practice Note (Chambers: Queen's Bench Division: New Procedure)* [1983] 1 All ER 1119).

In a county court, notice must normally be given at least two clear days before a hearing (CCR Order 13 r 2) but the court has the power to abridge time for service (and to extend time even after the time limit has expired (Order 13 r 4(1)). Interlocutory applications are usually heard by a district judge in chambers, though some are heard in open court and by a circuit judge, such as an application to break a fixture. If in doubt , ask at the court office before the hearing. Applications are made by way of originating application in form N244 on notice. If it is necessary to apply to adjourn on the day of an actual trial, the application will be heard by the trial judge. Further applications ancillary to an adjournment, eg for directions, can also be made at this stage.

In the High Court, a summons for directions must be taken out by the plaintiff within one month of the close of pleadings (RSC Order 25 r 1) and served at least 14 days before the hearing. Any party may apply for directions at any stage under this order but the bulk of the directions should be applied for by the initial summons (RSC Order 25 r 7). Other *inter partes* chambers applications must be made by summons (RSC Order 32) and usually two days notice is required (RSC Order 32 r 3), except in the case of applications for an extension or abridgement of time which may be served the day before the hearing. Some interlocutory applications must be served more than two days before the hearing such as applications for summary judgment and interim payment.

NOTES:

In the High Court, most short interlocutory applications are heard by a master and are made by summons. In London (at the Royal Courts of Justice), summonses that are expected to take less than 20 minutes are heard in the 'ordinary list' at 10.30, 11.00 and 11.30 am. Short summonses attended by counsel will be listed after 12.00 noon. Applications in the 'ordinary list' are heard in the masters' rooms, which lead off from the 'Bear Garden'. Summonses likely to take longer than 20 minutes are heard by 'private room appointment'. In certain circumstances or in cases of real urgency, the matter can be bought before a judge in chambers in the Queen's Bench Division. Examples of applications that must be made to a judge are applications for interlocutory injunctions and leave to apply for judicial review. Consult the text of Order 32 r 11 and the relevant practice directions for a full list of applications which will normally or always be heard by a judge. Applications to the judge will usually be in the general list if they are likely to take less than 30 minutes and in the chambers warned list if there is a longer time estimate. (See *Practice Direction (Judge in Chambers: Amended Procedure) The Times*, 16 October 1996). In the Chancery Division, masters can deal with all applications except those listed in RSC Order 32 r 14 and s 13 of the *Practice Direction (Chancery Division)*, 9 April 1991). As in the Queen's Bench Division, applications to the master are made by summons. Applications to the judge are made by notice of motion and are heard in open court (see s 15 of the *Practice Direction (Chancery Division)*, 9 April 1991). The practice in district registries will vary considerably and there is a greater likelihood of matters being listed before the judge.

In both county court and High Court, the judge hears appeals on interlocutory applications from a district judge or master.

NOTES:

Procedure for all interlocutory applications is relatively standard. We do not propose to deal with every single type of application but instead to give examples of four types of application in different courts on an *ex parte* and *inter partes* basis which we hope can be adapted for most situations:

(a) Summary judgment;

(b) Interlocutory injunction;

(c) Directions;

(d) Adjournments.

Apart from the rules and notes in the *Green Book* and *White Book,* you may also find it useful to refer to Barnard and Houghton's, *The New Civil Court in Action,* 1993: Butterworths; and O'Hare and Hill, *Civil Litigation,* 7th edn, 1996: FT Law and Tax.

Summary judgment

A plaintiff (or defendant on a counterclaim) can apply for summary judgment (to enter judgment without the need for a full trial) on the grounds that there is no defence to the claim. The procedure is governed by CCR Order 9 r 14 and RSC Order 14. If there is plainly no defence (for example, the defence is a point of law which is clearly misconceived or where the defendant's evidence is self-contradictory), judgment will be entered for the plaintiff. If there is no defence but there is a valid counter-claim, then judgment may be entered in respect of the plaintiff's claim with a stay of execution pending the trial of the counter-claim. Where there is a questionable or 'shadowy' defence and the court is very nearly prepared to give judgment for the plaintiff but not quite, the defendant will probably be given leave to defend, subject to a condition such as making a payment into court. If there is a clearly triable issue or fair probability

NOTES:

of a defence, then the defendant will be given unconditional leave to defend. If the application for summary judgment was clearly inappropriate, the plaintiff's application will be dismissed (for example, if the plaintiff knew that there was a genuine dispute or defence). The court might also enter judgment and assess the damages on a separate occasion (if damages are unliquidated) so long as the issues of liability and quantum can be separated.

Certain claims cannot be judged summarily. See CCR Order 9 r 14(1)(a) and RSC Order 14 r 1(2) for a full list. They include proceedings commenced by originating summons or petitions in the High Court and in a county court small claims, claims for possession of land (although there is a special procedure for claims against trespassers under Order 24 (see Chapter 7)).

In the High Court, an application can be made at any time after service of the statement of claim and the filing of a notice of intention to defend. The application is by summons supported by an affidavit and will usually be heard by a master. The summons and affidavit must be served at least 10 days before the hearing.

In a county court, an application can be made any time after a defence has been filed. The application is made by notice again supported by an affidavit and will usually be heard by a district judge. The summons and affidavit must be served seven days before the hearing.

The defendant may serve an affidavit in reply; if so, this must normally be done three days before the hearing. This a practice requirement rather than a rule.

The application

Where? High Court/county court

NOTES:

Who?   Master/district judge/judge

Robes?   No

Preliminaries

If appearing for the applicant, make sure that the affidavit in support sets out the relevant facts and explains why there is no defence or triable issue. If there is a dispute as to facts or a real issue between the parties, the defendant will be given leave to defend even if he or she is unlikely to succeed: the purpose of summary judgment proceedings is not to try the issues but to establish whether there are any issues. If acting for the respondent, consider what reasons can be put forward for a trial. Is there a dispute on the facts? Is it necessary for discovery to take place before you can fully consider the strength of the defence? Is it necessary to contact an important witness who could assist with the defence? If the dispute can only be resolved by hearing oral evidence, leave to defend will almost always be granted.

Hearing

(Defended application before a master in the High Court)

The hearing will take place in the master's room. Parties will be seated. Advocates should sit at the desk closest to the master's desk. Begin by introducing parties, nature of application and documents.

> *May it please you, master, this is my application for summary judgment. My learned friend Mr Rose appears for the defendant. A writ and statement of claim dated 17 June 1993 were served on 19 June 1993. A defence was filed on 15 July 1993. You will see that the plaintiff is claiming liquidated damages in the sum of £55,000 arising out of the defendant's alleged failure to pay for televisions supplied by the plaintiff to the defendant. The defence alleges that the televisions*

NOTES:

are incapable of receiving English programmes and, therefore, there is a total, or in the alternative, a partial failure of consideration. Master, an affidavit was sworn by Mr Rogers on behalf of the plaintiff company on 5 August 1993 and an affidavit in reply was sworn by Mr Davis of the defendants on 12 August 1993. Have you had an opportunity to consider these affidavits or would you like me to take you through them?

Refer the master to the chronology if one has been prepared or take him through the history set out in the affidavits for the significant dates. Point out any areas of disagreement about the history of events.

Master, there are a number of letters exhibited to the documents and a number of transactions alleged to have taken place. I have prepared a chronology and if it would assist I could hand that up. I have shown the document to my friend; whilst we were able to agree the majority of dates there are a couple of disagreements and perhaps I could point these out now. Firstly, the defendant denies that there was any telephone call between the parties on 7 June 1992 and secondly, he asserts that he sent a letter to the plaintiff on the 9 September, the alleged contents of which are referred to in Mr Davis' affidavit and no doubt we shall come to that later. He cannot produce a copy and the plaintiff refuses to accept that such a letter was sent and he certainly denies that he received such a letter. Master, would you prefer that I go through the chronology or would you like a moment or two to read it?

Next, the applicant should make submissions referring to the affidavits and documents. The respondent then makes submissions and the applicant may be invited to respond.

It is impossible to set out a full list of possible submissions but here are some tips:

NOTES:

(a) Let your opponent know if you are intending to refer to any cases. If you are going to refer to a lot of cases or anything particularly unusual, give your opponent and possibly the court at least 24 hours' notice of the references. Otherwise, take two copies with you to court, one for the court and one for your opponent.

(b) Make a note of the page and paragraph numbers to which you will refer the court.

(c) Remember that the test is not simply whether you are going to succeed at trial but whether there is a triable issue.

(d) The longer the argument, the more likely the defendant is to succeed. In the Queen's Bench, for example, if an application is expected to last more than half a day it will not be set down without the consent of the defendant or leave from a master.

(e) If acting for the defendant, emphasise the need for oral evidence, if possible; if for the plaintiff, emphasise the written evidence or lack of it and its inconsistency with the defendant's case.

Unless the master reserves judgment, which is unlikely, he will give his decision there and then. The possible orders have already been discussed. Take a careful note of the judgment in case the matter goes to appeal as masters' judgments are not tape recorded. Then deal with costs. If the plaintiff wins, the defendant will almost certainly have to pay the defendant's costs. Otherwise, the most likely order will be for costs in the cause. However, if the plaintiff's application clearly should not have been made and is dismissed, costs will be awarded against the plaintiff. Counsel should ask for a certificate.

NOTES:

What if ...?

You are acting for the plaintiff and the defendant attends at court with an affidavit?

The defendant is expected to serve the affidavit in reply three days before any hearing. If he or she has not done this but wants to rely on an affidavit produced on the day of the hearing, the plaintiff has two choices. If the affidavit discloses new evidence or makes new assertions, the plaintiff may need some time to consider the affidavit. In that case, he or she should ask for an adjournment with costs. If the affidavit does no more than set out in writing the defendant's case, then there may be no need for an adjournment and the hearing can proceed. The plaintiff will have to balance the benefit of a chance to consider the affidavit in greater detail against the benefit of getting on with the application, which is often a very important consideration in summary judgment applications.

Your witness informs you that there have been further relevant incidents since the affidavit was sworn?

Tell your opponent the gist of your assertions before you go into court (write them out in list form if there is time) and then tell the court when going through your evidence. If the court requires/allows you to do so, call your witness to give sworn evidence of the developments. Alternatively, write out a short supplemental affidavit which your client can swear at the court office (or the client can undertake to swear the affidavit if there is no time before the hearing).

The defendant does not attend and is not represented?

The court is very likely to order judgment to be entered in favour of the plaintiff so long as he or she can show that the summons and affidavit have been served. A plaintiff should always prepare an affidavit of service if the documents are

NOTES:

served personally; this can be filed if the defendant does not attend. If there is no affidavit of service, look for any other evidence indicating that the defendant has been served, for example, a letter from the defendant referring to the summons.

Interlocutory injunctions

An application for an interlocutory injunction is usually made after the issue of proceedings, whether or not an injunction was claimed in the pleadings. In cases of real emergency, it can be made before issuing proceedings (the applicant may be required to give an undertaking to issue proceedings straightaway).

In the High Court, the application is by summons or motion (see RSC Order 29 r 1(2)) (standard forms have recently been devised: see *Practice Direction (Interlocutory orders for injunctions) The Times*, 31 October 1996). In a county court, the application must be made on the prescribed form N16A.

In both courts, except in cases of real emergency, the application should be accompanied by an affidavit and a copy of the draft minute of order. The affidavit must explain the cause of action against the defendant, why an interlocutory injunction is needed and state the terms of the order sought (*Practice Note* [1983] 1 WLR 433). The application and affidavit should be served on the respondent at least two days before the hearing. An affidavit of service should generally be prepared and filed if the respondent fails to attend. See the beginning of this chapter for the rules on the contents of affidavits on *ex parte* applications. An *ex parte* order will normally only last for as long as it takes to bring the matter back on an *inter partes* basis. In a county court, applications are heard by a judge unless the district judge has trial

NOTES:

jurisdiction (eg cases with a value below £5,000, see Order 21 r 5), or is given jurisdiction specifically, as by the Family Proceedings Rules to hear applications for non-molestation and ouster orders. In the High Court, most applications will be heard by a judge.

In a county court, *inter partes* applications are heard in open court with a few exceptions, such as family matters (Order 13 r 6). *Ex parte* applications are almost always heard in chambers (Order 13 r 1(4)).

In the Queen's Bench Division of the High Court, all applications are heard in chambers. In the Chancery Division, they are always heard in open court.

The principles to be applied in applications for interlocutory injunctions are set out in the judgment of the House of Lords in *American Cyanamid v Ethicon* [1975] AC 396. The applicant should remember that, if an injunction is granted, he will probably be required to give an undertaking as to damages (this is not the practice in family cases not involving money), but it is implicit in the application even if not specifically extracted. See also Chapter 5.

The application

Where?	High Court/county court
Who?	Judge; possibly master or district judge (see above)
Robes?	No, if in Queen's Bench Division, *ex parte* applications (unless in the Chancery Division) or other chambers business, eg family cases. Yes in all other cases and always in the Chancery Division.

NOTES:

Preliminaries

In an *inter partes* application, check that all the necessary documents have been filed with the court and served on the other side. If the other side is present, see if it is possible to reach a settlement or define some of the issues. Quite often it is possible to compromise with undertakings being offered. If so, you must remember that in a county court any undertakings should be recorded on Form N117. The court will usually expect the order required and/or undertakings to have been written out before you go into court (CCR Order 13 r 6(6)). In the High Court, the successful party draws up the order after the hearing, although it may well be helpful to have a draft to show to the court.

Hearing

Ex parte application before a judge in the High Court

Introduce yourself and explain what your are applying for. Explain who the parties are and say what documents have been filed or hand them up.

> *May it please your Lordship, I appear on behalf of Eezy Fashions Limited. My Lord this is an ex parte application for an interlocutory injunction to restrain a company called Denim Diamonds Limited from launching a range of denim jeans called Colour Casuals. Denim Diamond intend to launch these jeans at a fashion launch at the Harrovian hotel tomorrow morning and the applicant seeks to restrain them from doing so on the grounds that the design of this particular type of jean is patented by them, and such a launch would make their patent worthless. No writ has yet been issued but I am able to offer an undertaking that one will be issued forthwith. An affidavit in support of this application has been prepared by the managing director of the Applicant, a Mr James Boyle, sworn today. That affidavit along with a draft minute of order should now be before your Lordship.*

Notes:

Then go through the background in greater detail, referring to the affidavit and chronology, if prepared. Otherwise, summarise the background history and give the court the main dates.

> *Has your Lordship had an opportunity to read the affidavit? May I briefly run through the background to this case. Paragraph 3 of Mr Boyle's affidavit explains the businesses of the two companies involved. The applicants make jeans for both sexes. They were only incorporated two years ago. The respondents make various denim fashions but concentrate on the jeans market. They have been in business for over 12 years. Last year, the applicant designed a new type of jeans: a denim jean that was able to change colour according to the weather. This design was patented in December of last year. It is this design that the applicants are alleging the respondent has copied.*

Next, explain the reasons for the urgent application.

> *This application is made ex parte because the launch takes place tomorrow and in the circumstances it was impossible to give the respondent the requisite notice. Unfortunately, the applicant only discovered the details of the launch this morning. It has been highly secret up until today. However, this morning an article was published in the Daily Dodge newspaper stating that tomorrow's event was 'to launch a new hyper-colour jean similar to the one on the market produced by Eezy Fashions'. Immediately upon reading that article, Mr Boyle telephoned the respondent company for an explanation. As he states at paragraph 5, he spoke to Mr Howe, the respondent company's managing director who confirmed that a similar jean to that currently produced by the applicants was to be launched but denied that it infringed the patent and refused to call off the launch. Consequently, the*

NOTES:

applicant had no option but to make this urgent application without notice.'

Then take the judge through the affidavit and make your submissions. These should be based on the principles of *American Cyanamid* and other relevant cases and show that:

(a) there is a serious issue to be tried;

(b) the loss likely to be incurred is more than financial loss;

(c) should the plaintiff fail, ultimately, the defendant will be adequately compensated in damages;

(d) the balance of convenience lies in the plaintiff's favour.

After explaining the reasons why there should be an order, go through the terms of the order you are asking for. If the order is granted costs are normally reserved. If the court is not prepared to grant an order but accepts that there is some urgency you should ask that time for service of the *inter partes* summons be abridged and for the application to be listed for hearing within a short period of time. Whatever the outcome, do not forget to ask for a certificate for counsel, if appropriate.

What if ...?

You are instructed by a party who has had an *ex parte* order made against them?

It is always possible to apply to vary or discharge an order, either on an *ex parte* or *inter partes* basis (CCR Order 37 r 2 and RSC Order 32 rr 5 and 6). An affidavit in support must be filed and for all other purposes the same rules as apply to the application for an injunction apply to this form of application. If the other side knew facts which have not been disclosed, you should consider asking for costs on an indemnity basis or even a wasted costs order, depending on the circumstances.

NOTES:

Directions

Directions appointments have two main purposes: firstly, to set a timetable for the substantive action and any interlocutory steps or applications; secondly, to enable the court, and often the parties, to take stock of the proceedings and consider whether the case is ready for trial and the state of the evidence.

In actions begun by writ in the High Court (except personal injury actions), RSC Order 25 r 1 requires the plaintiff to issue a summons within one month of the close of pleadings requiring the defendant to attend a directions appointment before the master. The summons will list a number of directions and the plaintiff will strike out those paragraph numbers which do not need to be dealt with and the defendant can, on notice served seven days before the hearing, ask for other matters to be dealt with. The standard form of summons lists various possible directions, including:

(a) consolidation with other pending cases;

(b) trial by Official Referee or master;

(c) transfer to the county court;

(d) leave to amend the writ or pleadings;

(e) further and better particulars of pleadings;

(f) discovery and inspection;

(g) disclosure and exchange of evidence, including expert evidence;

(h) mode of trial.

At the summons for directions by RSC Order 38 r 2A(2), the court is required to direct that witness statements must be exchanged 14 weeks before trial (and it may do so at any stage). In theory, this time limit cannot be varied simply by

NOTES:

agreement between the parties; the court's leave is required (RSC Order 38 r 10). In personal injury cases, automatic directions apply (RSC Order 25 r 8). If other directions are required or the timetable needs to be varied, a summons for specific directions can be issued. Rule 9 provides that in Chancery actions where the parties agree that the matter is to be tried by judge alone and set down within the six months and no other directions are needed, they can dispense with the summons for directions.

In a county court, automatic directions will apply in most cases (CCR Order 17 r 11). This rule sets out a default timetable for the case and time will begin to run at the deemed close of pleadings. The meaning of this expression has caused many practitioners considerable headaches and it has spawned a huge volume of cases. The position is much clearer now and the relevant cases should be consulted.

Again, if either of the parties wants other directions, they can apply for them on notice. Automatic directions do not apply in some cases, most importantly in possession actions and actions for the delivery up of goods. In these cases, there will be usually be a pre-trial review after close of pleadings when directions will be given. Parties should try to apply for all the directions they need at this hearing.

In automatic directions cases, witness statements should be exchanged within 10 weeks of the start of the timetable but this time limit may be extended by agreement between the parties or with leave of the court. In non-automatic directions cases, the procedure is set out at CCR Order 20 r 12A and is similar to the High Court procedure except that the usual time limit is 10 weeks.

NOTES:

The application

Where?	High Court /county court
Who?	High Court – master/district judge (district registries) County court – district judge
Robes?	No (unless directions are being sought at what should be the final hearing of an open court matter)

Preliminaries

Too often hearings are dismissed as 'just' directions appointments but their importance should not be underestimated. There are plenty of traps for the unwary advocate with little trial experience. Whilst the vast majority of directions appointments are not contentious, the court simply being asked on the attendance of one of the parties to approve an agreed order, if you are instructed to attend court especially on an *inter partes* basis, it is usually a sign of trouble. Many courts are now taking a very much more active interest in the steps leading up to trial and may not be satisfied with any agreement reached between the parties' representatives.

The Woolf Report recommends that in future there should be a fast-track trial procedure for claims worth between £3,000 and £10,000 (with the option of transfer out of the fast-track to the multi-track in certain cases, and vice versa for claims above the guideline limit). It is proposed that there will be a set timetable of 20–30 weeks, limited discovery, three-hour hearings, no oral evidence from experts and fixed costs.

This should mean that in fast-track cases there will not be directions hearings, except to vary the timetable imposed (and to do this applications will have to be made *before* the

NOTES:

time limit has passed). In multi-track cases, there will be a case management conference shortly after the defence is filed, and a pre-trial review about eight to 10 weeks before the final hearing. Solicitors will be expected to attend the case management conference and the pre-trial review (if not instructing counsel) and counsel the pre-trial review, if instructed. Clients will be expected to attend both hearings. Case management will be even more crucial and a thorough knowledge of the case will be necessary.

Examine the papers to see what directions orders have been made and whether they have been complied with. Consider what additional directions would be helpful to your client or if any of the target dates need to be varied. If there has been non-compliance, make sure you know why so that you can explain it to the court and apologise, if necessary. This can be of critical importance if the time for setting down for trial is looming and the case is not ready.

If there is time, arrange for a further application to be made and listed together with the hearing already arranged or at least see if the other side can be contacted and their agreement obtained. Even if a direction has not been formally applied for it may be possible to put something forward by consent or ask the court to dispense with the formal application (CCR Order 13 r 2; RSC Order 25 r 2). In the High Court, this may not be allowed, and in either court it will not be if the direction sought is vigorously opposed and will take longer than the time allowed.

Some examples to consider include whether there should be an experts meeting, whether the experts should be asked to deal with specific issues, whether some form of Scott Schedule or other way of presenting evidence should be specifically provided for, whether specific discovery is

NOTES:

required, whether specific provision is needed for the attendance of certain witnesses, what is the time estimate for the final hearing and whether there should be a split trial.

If part of the purpose of the directions hearing is to fix a date for trial, make sure that you know about witness availability.

It is rare for affidavit evidence to be necessary on a directions hearing, but it can be useful, for example, to show that expert evidence is necessary and/or the number and type of experts, or to give some explanation for delay in complying with automatic directions and/or the need for an extension of time for setting down, or why specific discovery is necessary.

The court has power to attach a condition that unless a direction is complied with the action will be struck out (an 'unless' or 'peremptory' order). There are several relevant rules in the High Court (eg RSC Order 25 r 6(3)) which are applied to the county court by s 76 of the County Courts Act 1984. Further specific powers in relation to the failure to provide particulars of pleadings are set out in CCR Order 13 r 2. An unless order must be carefully worded: see *Practice Direction (Peremptory Orders: Form)* [1986] 2 All ER 576.

Hearing

We will go through various different situations.

(A) Agreed directions; attendance by plaintiff; consent order/letter

Where the parties have agreed the directions in correspondence and only the plaintiff is attending, the advocate should very briefly outline the nature of the case and hand up the consent order/letter detailing the agreed directions.

NOTES:

Any unusual directions should be explained.

Master, I appear for the plaintiff in this matter. You will see from the statement of claim that this is an action for damages for the defendant surveyors' alleged negligent misstatement. The plaintiff purchased a holiday home in Majorca at a total cost of £130,000 which was valued by the defendants before purchase. He alleges that the house is in a very defective state and that it is of a substantially lower value than the amount at which the defendants' valued it and that he has lost income from being unable to let the property when he was not staying there. The defendant has denied that the valuation was negligent. Master, the pleadings were deemed to have been closed on 18 January and the parties have agreed directions. Could I hand up a letter from my instructing solicitors to the defendants' solicitors on 9 February setting out various directions. You will see that the letter has been signed by the defendant's solicitors to indicate their consent. Master, most of the directions agreed are, hopefully, self-explanatory but you will note that paragraph 7 provides for three experts' reports on each side. The reason for the greater number of experts than usual is that, in addition to reports from a builder as to the defects and a surveyor as to the property's value, a report will be needed from a travel agent as to the loss of profit caused by the plaintiff's inability to rent the home out to other holidaymakers.

Master, unless I can be of any further assistance I would ask for an order for directions in the terms set out in that letter.

(B) Automatic directions; further directions sought by one party; agreed by the other party

In a situation where automatic directions would apply but further directions are sought and agreed between the

NOTES:

parties, a similar approach to that set out in (A) above should be adopted, with an explanation why the automatic directions should be varied.

(C) Contested directions appointment

When one party has issued a summons for specific directions which have not been agreed, the advocate for that party should begin in the normal way by introducing the parties and the nature of the case, and then go on to say what directions are being sought and why. It is often helpful if the directions sought are written out and handed to the court.

> *Master, the plaintiff seeks a direction that this matter be tried by the Official Referee as there are many technical and detailed questions concerning the construction of the property that need to be addressed and these are more appropriate for the Official Referees Court. Master, you will see particulars of the alleged defects at paragraph 8 of the statement of claim. There are problems with the foundations of the building, the roof and the air conditioning system.*

The opposing party can then address the court on why the suggested direction should not be given, referring to facts and law as appropriate.

Costs

If directions are agreed, it is unlikely that a certificate for counsel will be granted. Costs will usually be in the cause. If the directions are not agreed, the costs order will depend on the balance of success. For example, if both parties have made applications which are refused or granted the order would most likely be costs in the cause.

NOTES:

What if ...?

At the trial of a hearing the other side ask for an adjournment which you are instructed to oppose?

As will be seen below, if an application for an adjournment has been successful, the court will usually want to make directions to ensure the case gets back to court as soon as possible. Even if you are instructed to oppose the request for an adjournment, you can, and should, nonetheless discuss the question of directions with your opponent and try to agree them subject to the court's decision on adjournment. This is very common in county court cases where automatic directions do not apply, for example, at the hearing of a possession action in the 'short possession' list where the defendant attends on the day and wants to defend the action.

Typical directions which might then be required are:

(a) plaintiff to file an amended particulars of claim within 14 days;

(b) defence to be filed 14 days thereafter;

(c) reply, if so advised 14 days thereafter;

(d) discovery by list 14 days thereafter;

(e) inspection seven days thereafter;

(f) exchange of witness statements 10 weeks before final hearing;

(g) experts' reports to be exchanged 10 weeks before final hearing (two experts only for each side);

(h) each party to notify the other party as to which witnesses are required to attend for the purposes of cross-examination four weeks before trial;

(i) case to be set down for final hearing by a circuit judge on

NOTES:

the first open date after 12 weeks with a time estimate of two days;

(j) final directions hearing 14 days before trial, before a circuit judge, time allowed 15 minutes.

Adjournments

A case may need to be adjourned at virtually any stage. If, for some reason, a hearing – whether interlocutory or final – cannot proceed, it may be adjourned even if it has already begun. Common reasons for needing an adjournment are:

(a) a witness is not available or has not turned up;

(b) the other side has not served an expert report or witness statement until shortly before the start of the trial;

(c) the expert cannot get the report ready in time;

(d) further time is needed to assess the progress of recovery from injuries, or the success of repairs carried out;

(e) there is a need to amend the pleadings significantly or respond to amended pleadings;

(f) the client has only just put solicitors in funds and necessary preparatory steps have not been taken.

Do not make the mistake of regarding a request for an adjournment as a pure formality. This is going to be even more true post-Woolf, at least in theory, assuming that the courts are going to be able to meet their listing commitments. As with any other application, the court will consider whether, on the law and the facts, you are entitled to your adjournment, and what order if any should be made as to costs. The power to adjourn is governed by CCR Order 13 r 3 (RSC Order 32 r 4, 35 r 3) and is a discretionary power. The crucial question is usually whether one party would be unfairly prejudiced by the grant or refusal of an adjournment. If the prejudice to the party resisting the adjournment can be compensated by an award of costs, the adjournment will be granted with costs against the party applying for it.

So, if you go to court intending to seek an adjournment, make sure that you have worked out what the consequences of the adjournment would be to both parties, and be prepared to argue that the balance falls in your favour. You should also be prepared to proceed with the hearing in the event that your application to adjourn fails. Quite a few courts are now adopting the practice of listing a final directions hearing shortly before the final hearing and if an application to adjourn has not been made at this stage the court is going to take a lot of convincing before granting an adjournment. You should also consider whether it is practical for the court to hear part of the case even if it cannot all be heard, eg liability but not quantum.

Finally, remember that adjournments can be made conditional. For example, a claim for possession of land where a tenant has not paid the rent may be adjourned on condition that the tenant pays the arrears. Advocates should be prepared to be inventive in thinking of conditions: extracting them from the other side can make it worthwhile for your client to submit to an adjournment; equally, submitting to conditions may get you the adjournment which your client needs.

The application

It is not possible to give guidance on whether robes should be worn or not or whether the matter will be heard in a county court or the High Court as this will depend on the nature of the substantive proceedings and the stage at which the application is made. One important point to note, however, is that an application to break a fixture will be heard in open court and usually by the judge. Such an application should of course be made as far as possible in advance of the date of the trial.

Hearing

There follows some examples of issues which often arise when requesting an adjournment.

(A) Requesting the adjournment; failure of witness to attend

Begin by introducing the parties and summarise the purpose of the application. Ask the judge if he has read the papers. Then ask for the adjournment and give your reasons. Remember that adjourning a matter on the date it has been set down for hearing means the court's time has been wasted and other litigants have been inconvenienced; therefore, be suitably apologetic if the adjournment could have been avoided.

> *May it please your Honour, I appear for the plaintiff in this matter, my learned friend Mr Fisher appears for the defendant. Your Honour, this was to have been my application for a mandatory injunction to order the defendant to remove a satellite dish she has erected on the property. Your Honour will have seen from the papers that the property has been let by the plaintiff to the defendant on an assured tenancy. Unfortunately, my witness Miss Flopsy, who was to have given evidence as to the tenancy agreement and the alleged breach, was taken ill this morning and will not be able to attend today. In the circumstances, I would ask for this matter to be adjourned to the first open date after 14 days. I do, of course, apologise to the court and to my learned friend for the inconvenience such an adjournment will undoubtedly cause. I am aware that this matter was listed for half a day's hearing, Your Honour, but without Miss Flopsy I would not be able to prove my case.*

NOTES:

(B) Period of the adjournment

You must be prepared to suggest, and justify, the length of any adjournment.

If you need only a very short adjournment, then it may be possible to apply for this through the usher. For example, if negotiations are taking place outside court but the judge is ready to hear the case, tell the usher that the parties are negotiating and how much more time is required. Either the usher will pass this on the judge, who will let you know whether he or she is prepared to wait, or the judge might want to see the advocates to get an idea of what is going on and whether the case is likely to settle so that it is safe to allow some extra time. Sometimes this can be a useful opportunity to get a hint from the judge about the way he or she is thinking which might assist the negotiations.

If an adjournment to another date is being sought but no further steps have to be taken between the date of the request and the next hearing (as when the only reason for the adjournment is the illness of a witness), you can ask the court to fix a particular date in the future. The judge may not have details of the available dates and you should ask at the court office for available dates before going into court; these can then be suggested to the judge.

> *Your Honour, I have taken the liberty of speaking to the court office and I am informed that the earliest available date for another half day hearing is 6 June.*

If very few steps have to be taken between the request for the adjournment and the next hearing, the case can be listed for hearing on the first open date after a certain period of time. For example, if a 'family' matter is to be adjourned for a report to be filed.

> *Your Honour, the Court Welfare Officer informs me that she needs a further two weeks to prepare her*

NOTES:

report. In that case, I would suggest that this matter be relisted for the first open date after 28 days, which will give the parties enough time to receive the report and digest its contents.

It may not be possible to fix the date if, for example, you are not sure how long it will take to get the matter ready for trial, or if witness availability is not known. However, it is increasingly common for the court to want to set the whole timetable as soon as possible. Sometimes the court will accept a direction that the case be 'set down for trial upon the filing of certificates of readiness from both parties' solicitors together with a time estimate'. Otherwise, it may prefer to fix a further directions appointment for the purpose of setting down, or direct that the parties notify the court about witness availability within a certain time frame, and so on.

(C) Costs

The most bitterly fought issue is often that of the costs of the adjournment rather than the adjournment itself. Aside from the question of prejudice, costs will often be awarded against the party whose 'fault' it is that the case cannot proceed. If this party is your client, search for any reasons why the costs should be reserved. If neither party is to blame, the costs will usually be in the cause.

What if ...?

You are instructed very late the night before a hearing?

Lack of preparation is not necessarily a good reason for an adjournment! You will be expected to have prepared as well as possible despite the lack of time available. Counsel has a duty not to return a brief without explaining the reasons to the instructing solicitor and not to withdraw from a case in circumstances where the client may be unable to find other assistance in time to prevent prejudice being suffered by the

NOTES:

client. If, however, you are not competent to take the brief but there is not enough time to put the hearing off, or you find that more information or evidence is necessary, you will have to explain this to your client and the court. Counsel should speak to their clerks and instructing solicitors to find out why the instructions were late or inappropriately allocated, bearing in mind the wasted costs provisions.

Your application to adjourn fails?

If the judge refuses the adjournment and you are required to proceed with the case, you will usually be allowed a short adjournment to obtain your clients' further instructions, if you ask nicely!

NOTES:

4 : The trial

> Trial: that which puts one to the test, especially, a painful test of one's endurance, patience or faith; hence, affliction, trouble, misfortune (*Shorter Oxford English Dictionary*).

The law is often criticised for moving at a snail's pace but it may not seem so slow to the advocate involved in a trial. This chapter deals with some of the skills you will need to develop to survive the experience.

The Woolf Report contains no specific proposals as to trial procedures but they will, of course, be affected by pre-trial reforms, particularly the fast-track cases. You are likely to have to restrict your questioning to key areas relating to agreed issues.

Although this chapter concentrates on trials in civil cases in the county court, the basic approach is similar in the High Court. We have also included a section dealing with arbitrations in the small claims court. By way of illustration, we shall proceed through a fictitious road traffic accident trial in the county court. These are the facts:

> *The plaintiff is a Mr Smith who was driving a Rover motor car. The defendant, Mr Jones, was driving a Jaguar. It is agreed that a collision did occur on 14 March 1991 at the junction of Easy Street and the A100. Mr Smith was attempting to pull out of Easy Street onto the A100. Easy Street is a minor road with a give-way sign. Mr Smith says that he stopped at the give-way sign and only proceeded after he saw Mr Jones flash his lights at him and indicate to turn left down Easy Street. Mr Jones admits he was driving along the A100 and that he flashed his lights but says that this was simply to warn Mr Smith not to proceed. He says that*

NOTES:

his indicator was certainly not on. Mr Smith claims damages for the cost of repairs to his vehicle and the loss of use of his motor vehicle.

Preliminaries

When the judge is called everyone in court should stand up. Legal representatives should bow to the judge and then sit down until the name of the case is called. Then the plaintiff's advocate should stand up, introduce himself and his opponent and open the case or, if there are any preliminary points such as amendments to pleadings or procedural defects, tell the court as much of the facts as are necessary to be able to deal with them. Ideally, the parties should have discussed this before the case. If the defendant has a preliminary application to make, the plaintiff's advocate should tell the judge and sit down. The defendant's representative then makes his application after which the plaintiff responds. Once the judge has ruled on the preliminaries, the plaintiff's representative can go on to open more fully.

Opening speeches

Opening speeches in civil trials of this size and complexity should be short and provide the judge with a brief introduction to the case. Initially, find out whether the judge has got the trial bundle, and whether they have read it. It is often only necessary to open by saying what the case is about and give a concise summary of the facts, the remedy sought, the heads of damage and whether the amount of damages is in dispute and to what extent. Sometimes, even this is not necessary if the judge has read the papers. If there is a counterclaim, this should also be referred to.

In road traffic accident cases, there is unlikely to be a very large bundle before the court but the court should be directed to any plans or photographs and informed as to

NOTES:

whether these are agreed and for what purpose they are agreed. For example, it may be agreed that a photograph should go into the bundle, as an aid to examination of the witnesses, but not agreed that it is an accurate representation of the accident scene. If the latter applies, you may need to call evidence to show when and how the photograph was taken and how, if at all, it differs from the scene at the time of the accident (eg whether there were road works or trees with leaves on, etc). In more complex cases, it may be necessary to take the judge through the bundle briefly explaining the relevance of the documents. Refer to the page numbers in the bundle when taking the judge to a particular document and remember to wait until the judge has found the particular document before explaining it.

Smith v Jones

Opening by the advocate for the plaintiff:

> *May it please your Honour, I appear for the plaintiff in this matter, and Mr Davis appears for the defendant.*
>
> *Your Honour, this is a claim arising from a road traffic accident on the 14th of March 1991 at the junction of Easy Street and the A100 at Parsnips Green. The plaintiff was driving his car, a green Rover 214, along Easy Street and was trying to join the A100, which is a dual carriageway, when the defendant who was driving his car, a dark red Jaguar, along the A100 crashed into him. The plaintiff claims special damages of £2,000 for the cost of repairs to his vehicle, and this sum has been agreed subject to liability. He also claims that as a result of that accident he suffered injuries to his leg and seeks to be compensated for those injuries and his subsequent loss of earnings. A medical report from his GP dated 25 March 1991 is at page five of the bundle and gives particulars of the injury.*

NOTES:

Your Honour, the defendant by his defence admits the fact of the accident but denies that he was negligent.

The bundle contains invoices and estimates of the cost of the repairs to Mr Smith's vehicle and numerous pay slips. Unless your Honour has any objections I do not propose to deal with these in opening but rather ask Mr Smith to explain them when he gives his evidence. There are, however, a number of photographs and a plan, which are agreed, and should probably be mentioned now. The plan is not to scale but shows the area in question. Photographs 1, 2 and 3 show the plaintiff's view at differing distances from the junction. Photographs 5 and 6 show the defendant's view along the A100.

That is all I have to say by way of opening and unless your Honour has any further questions I will call Mr Smith.

Examination-in-chief

The aim of the examination-in-chief is to make your witnesses relay their story as favourably as possible and to insulate them from cross-examination. When your witness is called, he or she will be required to take the oath or affirm. First, ask the witness for his or her name and address. If it is a witness of fact, the personal address should usually be given but expert witnesses, housing officers and the like should give their professional address. Next, refer the witness to his or her statements. Ask him or her to look it over and identify the signature at the end. Then ask whether he or she can confirm that the contents of the statement are true to the best of his or her knowledge and belief.

What happens next will vary greatly from case to case. Part of the purpose of witness statements is to save time at trial as well as to allow the other side to know what your case is.

NOTES:

In many road traffic cases, however, the judge feels that it is important to get an impression of the witness before cross-examination and will be perfectly happy for you to ask the witness to describe the accident in his or her own words. Many witnesses will not have given evidence before and need time to get used to the court room. You must strike a balance between keeping the trial to a reasonable length and helping the witness to relax.

Here are some points to consider:

(a) Deal with any matters which are missing from the witness's statement or any corrections which need to be made.

(b) Try to keep your questions brief and use plain English. For example, avoid the double negative which so many advocates seem attached to: 'would you not agree that it didn't in fact ...' etc. Avoid legal/police jargon and words such as subsequent, prior, proceeding, observe, occasion, recall. Make sure that you explain or get the witness to explain any terms of art particular to their trade or profession. Avoid compound questions: each question should deal with one point at a time.

(c) Structure your questioning: liability first, damages second. Under liability, cover: date, time, purpose of journey, weather conditions, traffic conditions, where the accident happened and where each vehicle was on the road. Tell the witness as you move from one segment to another. For example, 'I now want to ask you about the damage to your car'.

(d) Slow down when you come to an important point and develop it by breaking down your questions into short segments. When you want to emphasise a point stop asking questions beginning 'describe' or 'what

NOTES:

happened next'. For example, instead of asking the witness to describe how the collision occurred, break it down. 'Where was your car when you first saw the defendant's car? What colour was it? Were there any other cars on the road? Were there any cars parked at the side of the road? Where was the defendant's car when you first saw it? What speed were you travelling at? What speed was the defendant travelling' and so on.

(e) Tackle the weaknesses: of course there are going to be weaknesses in your case but, if these are glaringly obvious, it is often best to take your witness/es to these in their examination-in-chief; that way they will be able to take the sting out of your opponent's questions and it will allow them to mitigate that weakness, if at all possible. This is what is meant by insulating your case. Those weaknesses that are not so obvious can be left and dealt with in re-examination if raised by your opponent.

(f) Do not ask leading questions: a leading question is one which feeds the witness the answer. Questions which (i) require 'yes' or 'no' answers *and* (ii) pre-suppose certain facts in the question will tend to be leading questions. For example, the question 'You were wearing a seat belt, weren't you?' is a leading question whereas 'Were you wearing a seat belt?' is not. Generally, questions beginning 'who, what, where, why, when, how, explain, describe' will not be leading. Leading questions are not permitted in examination-in-chief except where the matter in question is not disputed in the pleadings or when it is sought to elicit a specific denial from the witness. When dealing with minor issues which are not particularly material to the crux of the case, it may be that your opponent will not mind you leading your witness. You should always confirm this with him or her

NOTES:

before asking leading questions. This can be done openly by saying, for example, 'I hope my learned friend does not object to my leading this witness on issues relating to his employment?'.

(g) Deal with all necessary issues: your witness must be asked questions on all issues on which he or she can comment and which you wish to put to your opponents witnesses or refer to in your closing. If there are any plans or documents which he must verify or explain, he should be directed to them: remember it is he or she who must give the evidence, not you. When introducing exhibits, once the witness has mentioned them, hand the exhibit over to the witness to identify. In road traffic accident cases, when asking witnesses to, say, locate the site of the accident on a plan, be careful; strictly speaking, once the witness has marked the plan, it should become an exhibit, though in practice judges overlook this technicality.

(h) Take notes: if you are examining your own witness, try to make notes of their answers: they can be used when making your closing speech. If your opponent is examining their witness-in-chief, you must take notes so that where necessary you can put the answers to the witness in cross-examination as well as referring to them in closing.

Smith v Jones

Plaintiff's advocate examining-in-chief Mr Smith:

I call Mr Smith

(Mr Smith will be required to give the oath or affirm.)

Can you give the court your full name and address?
What is your occupation?
Do you hold a full driving licence?

NOTES:

How long have you held that licence for?
Mr Smith, although I will be asking you questions, could you please direct your answers to his Honour.
Mr Smith, everyone here agrees that an accident occurred on 14 April last year but could you tell the court at what time you say that accident occurred?
What were the weather conditions like?
What was the condition of the road surface?
What was visibility like?
Moving to the accident itself, there should be a copy of a plan of the area at page five of the bundle in front of you. Can you hold that plan up and show the court exactly where you say the accident happened?
Which direction were you coming from? Where were you intending to go?
When did you first see the plaintiff's car? Was it moving or stationery?
Which direction was the plaintiff's car facing?
Mr Smith, there should be some photographs in the bundle in front of you at page 25. Could you tell the court which photographs best show your view as you were travelling along Easy Street?
Can you estimate what speed you were travelling at?
What were you intending to do upon reaching the junction?
Were there any road signs towards the end of Easy Street that joins the A100? ...

When you have finished your examination-in-chief, check your notes to be sure you have missed nothing out. If this will take more than a second or two, say:

Just wait a moment, please.

When you are sure there is nothing else, say:

Thank you, Mr Smith. Stay where you are while the defendant's representative asks you some questions.

NOTES:

Cross-examination

Cross-examination is the examination of your opponent's witnesses. It is about two main things: 'putting' your case and 'putting down' your opponent's case. You need to think about what the witness can do to help your case and what you can do to qualify or discredit their evidence.

Putting your case

It is an essential rule of evidence that you ask the witness questions on every part of your case on which that witness can speak and which is in dispute. If you do not ask the witness a question on any such topics, you will be treated as having accepted the other side's version and will not be allowed to contradict it in your closing speech. 'Putting your case' is often done by saying to the witness, 'I put it to you that (for example) you were not wearing a seat belt'. This is not the only way to do it, and some say that it is a clumsy and boring way. As long as you put the question to the witness in some form that he or she can answer, you will have 'put' that part of your case. 'The truth is you weren't wearing a seat belt' is quite adequate and may often be more effective. In cross-examination leading questions are perfectly permissible.

Putting down your opponent's case

To put down your opponent's case you have to find discrepancies and inconsistencies in the evidence. Advance your case by showing how weak the witness's evidence is. Do this by showing the limitations in the witness's testimony, for example, point out what the witness did *not* see rather than what they did see. Especially when dealing with eyewitnesses, attempt to show how the alleged sighting of the defendant, accident, etc may be mistaken, eg by pointing out the obstructions that were in the witness's line of vision,

NOTES:

how far away the witness was, poor visibility and so on. Examine peripheral issues: although some matters may seem incidental to the case it is often worth probing them if they could show inconsistencies in the testimony. However, you must balance this against the need to keep to time estimates and not go into too much depth on irrelevant aspects.

Cross-examination is often thought of as the most enjoyable part of a trial in that it entitles you to insult complete strangers without reservation. This is not the whole truth! Although you are free to ask leading questions, it is still a very technical and difficult art to master. Again, there are some 'rules' which we think should be observed:

(a) Be as polite as possible: there is very little to be gained by launching into a barrage of personal insults. Particularly when you are examining an independent or professional witness, you may well be prevented from doing this by the judge unless it is absolutely necessary. Of course, if the witness is being deliberately unhelpful and evasive, it may be necessary to speak in harsher tones but even then try to do so politely. For example, it is usually better to say, 'Do you really mean that?' rather than to say, 'You are lying aren't you?' (although you should not shrink from saying such things if they are necessary).

(b) Be patient: you may have a very good point to make, which will be very favourable to your case. Do not rush into making this point. Get the witness into a position where they cannot retract their statement. It is usually better to begin gently and try and lull the witness into a false sense of security before 'going for the jugular'. Let us take the common example of a plaintiff who says that he or she was severely shaken up after a road accident but managed to drive his car over a long distance to work and then spend the rest of the day working, and he

NOTES:

or she then took a week off from work a couple of days later:

Q: Do you have a good relationship with your employers?
A: Yes.
Q: Were they sympathetic when you took a week off from work the Wednesday following the accident?
A: Yes, they were sympathetic, they were very concerned because I was clearly shaken up.
Q: Were you very shaken up by the accident?
A: Terribly.
Q: Yes, I know the feeling; it feels as if you're not able to do anything right?
A: That's right.
Q: It becomes very difficult to concentrate doesn't it?
A: Yes.
Q: Then can you explain how, in your severely shaken up state when you were unable to do anything or to concentrate, you managed to drive to work, a distance of over 30 miles and then spend the remainder of the day concentrating on difficult tasks at work?

(c) Apply a logical structure: as with examination-in-chief your cross-examination should follow some sort of order. This does not necessarily have to be the order adopted by your opponent but it should be sufficiently logical so that the court and the witness knows which topic each series of questions relates to.

(d) Ask questions: it is very easy to fall into the trap of making comments as opposed to asking questions. This behaviour will quickly be reprimanded by the judge. Incorporate your comments into questions. Do not state that the witness acted unreasonably; put it in a question: 'Was that sensible/reasonable in the circumstances?'

NOTES:

(e) Take notes: you should make notes for the same reasons as suggested in the section on examination-in-chief.

Smith v Jones

Defendant's advocate cross-examining Mr Smith:

Q: Mr Smith, where were you coming from?
A: Home.
Q: And where were you going to?
A: Work.
Q: Do you know the A100 well?
A: Yes, I join it from Easy Street every day to get to work.
Q: So you have taken that route many times?
A: Many, certainly more times than your client.
Q: And so you know that it is usually a very congested road?
A: Of course.
Q: At what time do you say the accident occurred?
A: 8.45 am.
Q: And how far away were you from work at the point the accident occurred?
A: About 5 miles.
Q: Would you disagree with me if I said that it is in fact 6 miles?
A: Not at all.
Q: And as you have taken that route many times you know that at that time of the morning 6 miles along the A100 could take up to 20 to 25 minutes?
A: Yes.
Q: What time do you start work Mr Smith?
A: About 9.00 am.
Q: In fact, you are expected to start work exactly at 9.00 am aren't you? And this was especially true at the time of the accident as you had only started working two days ago, isn't that right?
A: Maybe it is but how is that relevant?
Q: It is relevant because the truth is that you were

NOTES:

exceptionally late for a new job and so you were in a hurry, isn't that right? And that is why you tried to pull out of Easy Street on to the A100 when there was very little space ...

Q: Mr Smith, you have held your licence for 15 years, would you describe yourself as an experienced driver?

A: Yes.

Q: One who obeys road signs and regulations?

A: Of course.

Q: And you take care to ensure you comply with the Highway Code?

A: Yes.

Q: Are you familiar with the Highway Code?

A: Relatively.

Q: As an experienced driver would you say that it is important to comply with the Highway Code?

A: Yes.

Q: Now you say that you pulled out because you saw Mr Jones indicating and flashing at you?

A: Yes and I stick by that.

Q: I have no doubt you do but do you know that your actions, even on your evidence, were contrary to the Highway Code?

A: I do not know what you mean.

Q: Perhaps I can help. Paragraph 111 of the Code says 'When waiting at a junction do not assume that a vehicle coming from the right and signalling left will do so. Wait and make sure'. Paragraph 136 says 'Flashing your headlights means only one thing – it lets another road user know you are there. Do not flash your head lamps for any other reason and never assume that it is a signal to proceed'. Now do you accept that your actions were not in accordance with the Highway Code?

NOTES:

Re-examination

The general rule regarding re-examination is, do not re-examine! Avoid the temptation of asking 'just one question' unless it is absolutely necessary. Remember that you are only entitled to ask questions *arising from your opponent's cross-examination*. So do not leave your best points to last because if they are not raised by your opponent you will not be entitled to make them. Remember that the same rules regarding leading questions apply to re-examination as do to examination-in-chief. Re-examination may be necessary where your opponent has highlighted inconsistencies in your witness's testimony or has elicited only the part of an event that is favourable to their case.

After you have concluded any re-examination, you should ask the judge if he or she has any questions. If so, both you and your opponent are entitled to re-examine the witness on any matters arising from the answers to the judge's questions. Once there are no more questions for the witness unless they are a party to the proceedings they may wish to leave the court. No witness should be released without the judge's permission. Simply ask: 'Your Honour, if there is no further need for this witness, may he or she be released?'

Closing speeches

You may dream of making 'the great closing speech', the one that will capture the attention and imagination of the audience, that will rescue a dying case, convert the unconverted ... and so on! Unfortunately, even if you have the ability to make such a speech, there is little opportunity to do so in the majority of cases. However, the aim remains the same, to persuade the audience that yours is the better case.

NOTES:

The defence makes the first closing speech. This should include a brief précis of the evidence given for both sides. Show the weaknesses in the plaintiff's case and stress the strengths of your case. Again, explain the weaknesses in your case. Make any legal submissions, using law reports or books if necessary. Always provide your opponent with a copy of any authorities you are proposing to use before the trial begins and bring copies for the judge. A common mistake amongst junior advocates is to repeat themselves many times in their closing. When in danger of doing this remind yourself that you are speaking to an experienced legal professional who will be able to pick up your points very quickly and will be bored by constant repetition. One technique is to summarise your submissions at the outset, giving them numbers, and then deal with each submission in order. It is helpful to prepare the speech in note form, so that the structure is clear to you before you begin. Invite the judge to dismiss the plaintiff's action and, if necessary, to find for the defendant on the counter-claim. The plaintiff's representative will make a shorter closing speech. He or she need not summarise the evidence in any great detail but should highlight disputed areas and offer alternative conclusions.

It is now becoming far more common for advocates to exchange 'skeleton' arguments prior to a trial and to provide a copy for the judge. Skeletons should summarise the submissions you intend to make, referring to cases and statutes where appropriate, and should not be a transcript of your entire closing speech. When making your closing speech take the judge through your skeleton, expanding on each point orally. Skeletons have the advantage of focussing the advocate's mind and encouraging him to proceed logically, as well as reducing the length of the judge's note.

NOTES:

Smith v Jones

Closing speech by defendant's advocate:

> *... Your Honour has heard the evidence and I hope that the summary I have given is an accurate and fair one. It is the defendant's case that the plaintiff pulled out when it was not safe for him to do so and that in so doing he caused the accident. Of course, the plaintiff says that he was not indicating as he approached the turning into Easy Street but, in my submission, even if your Honour finds against the plaintiff on that point, he cannot have been the only person responsible for the accident; at the very least, the defendant should be held to have been contributory negligent. I base this submission on three points and it may be helpful if I summarise these at the outset: (a) The defendant acted contrary to the Highway Code; (b) Considering the busy traffic conditions the defendant should have exercised greater caution; and (c) The weight of authority I shall put before your Honour suggests that in such cases there must be a substantial reduction for contributory negligence ...*

Judgment and afterwards

Always take a good note of the judgment, in case of appeal.

After judgment has been given, it is usual to deal with the questions of costs and interest. Where one party has clearly succeeded, the judge will usually ask the other party why costs should not be awarded against them. Where the question of costs is not quite so clear it will usually be for the plaintiff's/applicant's advocate to address the court first but there is no fixed rule and the court will usually allow you to reply to any particular points which you did not cover.

You will need to calculate interest due on the judgment if you have not been able to do so before you go into court. For

NOTES:

this reason it is important always to take a calculator. The judge will usually ask for the total sum of interest and the rate of interest which has been used. The advocate for the plaintiff should tell the judge what their calculations are. If the judge simply adopts the plaintiff's figures, the advocate for the defendant may address the court on the question of the interest rate used or the calculation if appropriate.

Small claims arbitration

If the amount claimed in the particulars of claim is less than £3,000, the case will automatically be referred to arbitration in the county court as a small claim (unless it is a possession action or personal injury action over £1,000). The district judge may, however, order such a case to be tried in open court if he or she is satisfied of any one of the following:

(a) that the claim involves a difficult question of law or complicated facts;

(b) there is an allegation of fraud;

(c) due to the size of the counterclaim, the subject matter or the interests of third parties it would be unreasonable to deal with it as an arbitration; or

(d) both parties consent to a trial.

If both parties agree, even claims for more than £3,000 can be dealt with in the small claims court.

The rules governing arbitrations are to be found at Order 19 of the County Court Rules. Order 19 r 6 provides a cut down and speedy procedure and many of the normal rules are specifically disapplied as are the strict rules of evidence. The hearing usually takes place in a room at the county court and will be informal with all parties seated around a table except perhaps when a witness is being sworn. Neither the

NOTES:

judge nor the advocates are robed. It is likely the judge or the usher will tell the parties where they are to sit; if not, the plaintiff's advocate should sit in the seat closest to the judge's right and the plaintiff should sit next to them. The defendant and his or her representative should sit directly opposite. If counsel is attending with a solicitor, the solicitor sits next to counsel. Witnesses should wait outside unless the judge says that they can come into the room.

The order of speeches, or even the order of the examination of the witnesses may be varied by the district judge. The usual course of events is as follows. The plaintiff's advocate will give an introduction to his or her case and go through the bundle explaining any documents that require explanation. The procedure is then the same as with an open court trial in that the plaintiff's representative will call and examine their witnesses and the defendant's advocate will cross-examine them. The defendant's witnesses will then be called and examined-in-chief and cross-examined. The district judge may ask questions of any of the persons involved. Short speeches will then be made, with the defendant's representative going first. The district judge will then give judgment and make any necessary orders; a note should be taken of the judgment.

Litigants are often not represented in arbitrations and you should be careful not to place undue pressure on them outside court. Be prepared to ask questions and make submissions in a relatively non-legalistic manner: see the guidance given in Chapter 2.

At arbitration hearings, the court will only make an order for costs against a losing party if that party has acted unreasonably in their conduct of the case. Otherwise, the only costs that can be reclaimed are the costs of issuing the

NOTES:

summons and witness expenses. A fixed amount of £260 can be awarded if there is a claim for an injunction. Currently, the courts are awarding a maximum of £50 in respect of ordinary witnesses expenses for loss of earnings and £200 in respect of the expenses of an expert (plus reasonable travelling and overnight costs in both cases). An award for these expenses should be requested. There is no discretion to exceed these sums.

NOTES:

5 : Family law

This chapter will examine three areas of family law:

(a) domestic violence;

(b) ancillary relief; and

(c) Children Act applications.

Reference should also be made to Chapter 6, 'Contempt of Court'.

In family cases, especially disputes over children, the advocate must exploit a range of skills over and above those required in other fields. Emotions run high but the advocate must avoid fanning the flames, bearing in mind that the parties may have to live with each other afterwards. It is also important to try to keep issues over money and children separate, which is not always easy for the client to understand.

The advocate in a family case is not a social worker but clients will require a high degree of sensitivity and sympathy because of the deeply personal nature of the issues. It will usually be necessary to allow extra time for conferences and negotiations. More than ever the advocate needs to be aware of practicalities such as who can look after the children while the parties are at court.

An extremely useful book to take to court with you which covers all three of the above areas is 'The Family Court Practice 1996', in District Judge Cleary (ed), *Family Law*, 1995, Jordan Publishing. This contains procedural summaries of every conceivable family application and the main statutes and rules of court.

NOTES:

Domestic violence

This section will deal primarily with applications related to violence within marriage or cohabitation. Brief reference will be made to tortious injunctions of a similar nature between other members of the family, neighbours, etc and see also the section on injunctions in Chapter 4.

Most applications are settled with the respondent agreeing to give an undertaking to the court in the terms of the injunction sought. If an undertaking is breached, the court has exactly the same powers of enforcement as if an injunction has been made but a power of arrest cannot be attached to an undertaking. An undertaking does not involve any admissions as to past conduct, nor does the judge make any findings of fact.

Injunctions can be obtained *ex parte* but only if circumstances make it impossible or dangerous to give notice to the respondent. An *ex parte* order will usually last for only a week. As always, full and frank disclosure of all known relevant facts is essential and the affidavit should explain the reason for going *ex parte*.

In general, although courts will usually be willing to grant non-molestation injunctions, it is only in extreme cases that a respondent can be excluded from his or her home. Real danger of serious harm to the applicant or a child (usually violence, but exceptionally, emotional/psychological harm) must be shown. An ouster order is seldom, if ever, granted *ex parte*. *Ex parte* applications often request both a non-molestation and ouster order but it will usually be sensible not to pursue the ouster.

Inter partes orders should really only be made for a period of three months in the first instance (*Practice Note* [1978] 2 All

NOTES:

ER 1056). In practice, the courts will often impose orders for longer than this to save the parties from having to come back to court repeatedly.

Note also that under ss 144 and 148 Housing Act 1996, a 'social landlord' can seek possession of property let to one or both partners, where one partner has left because of violence or threats by the other (or the other's relative) and is unlikely to return.

Jurisdiction

The various courts have jurisdiction to grant injunctions in matrimonial matters in the following circumstances.

High Court and county court

(1) Within divorce proceedings;

(2) In relation to any application under the Children Act 1989, where the injunction sought is relevant to the care of the child concerned;

(3) Ancillary to a claim for damages in tort;

(4) In wardship proceedings;

(5) Under the Domestic Violence and Matrimonial Proceedings Act 1976 (DVMPA).

Magistrates' courts

Under the Domestic Proceedings and Magistrates' Courts Act 1978.

Types of order

Domestic Violence and Matrimonial Proceedings Act 1976

The Domestic Violence and Matrimonial Proceedings Act 1976 (DVMPA) is the most common jurisdiction for such applications, and in many ways the most versatile. It applies both to spouses and to unmarried cohabitees (of different

NOTES:

sexes), though the latter must have been living together at the time of the alleged misconduct. It provides for orders to:

(a) restrain one party from 'molesting' the applicant or a child living with the applicant: this covers a multitude of sins, but the usual wording of the order is 'assault, harass, pester or otherwise interfere with';

(b) exclude the respondent from the matrimonial home or a part of it or an area containing the matrimonial home;

(c) require the respondent to permit the applicant to enter and remain in the matrimonial home or a part of it.

In addition, where the respondent has caused *actual bodily harm* to the applicant or the child concerned, and is considered likely to do so again, a power of arrest can be attached to the order. This power is granted sparingly and usually for a three month period only. It is particularly useful as a support to orders forbidding the respondent from entering property which would not otherwise be a criminal offence. Whether or not a power of arrest can be attached, it is often a good idea for the applicant to contact the local domestic violence unit anyway and put them in the picture.

Divorce proceedings

If divorce proceedings are pending or are about to be commenced, both the High Court and the county court have jurisdiction to make injunctions in addition to their DVMPA jurisdiction by virtue of s 38 of the County Courts Act 1984 and s 37 of the Supreme Court Act 1981. An application for an ouster injunction should really be made under the Matrimonial Homes Act 1983. Unfortunately that Act cannot prevent someone from returning to the property or the area and so it may well be necessary to invoke the divorce or DVMPA jurisdiction.

NOTES:

Under s 1(2) of the MHA, the court can make an order:

(a) declaring, enforcing, restricting or terminating either spouse's rights of occupation; or

(b) prohibiting, suspending or restricting the exercise of such rights; or

(c) requiring either spouse to permit the other to exercise such rights.

This Act is not applicable to cohabitees.

Children Act 1989

An injunction under the DVMPA may order that a party be forbidden to molest, etc a child living with the applicant. If an order specifically relating to a child is sought the interests of that child are paramount. This will not apply to applications under the Matrimonial Homes Act.

In some cases, a prohibited steps order can achieve similar results to an injunction in terms of protecting a child but, where a s 8 order is granted, the court can also make an injunction. So, if a residence order is made, it can be accompanied by an order restraining a party from using violence towards the child. A prohibited steps order can be used to prevent a child from being removed from home. However, the use of violence against a parent can only be restrained by injunction (as it does not involve a step which could be taken by the parent in meeting his parental responsibility). A separate application, eg under the DVMPA 1976, must be made if such an order is required.

Procedures for ordering the return of a child who has been taken in breach of a residence order are complex and outside the scope of this book. Reference should be made to the relevant sections of McFarlane, H, *Children Law and Practice*, Jordan Publishing, the Family Law Act 1986 and the Child Abduction and Custody Act 1985, as appropriate.

NOTES:

Wardship

The court can grant injunctions to protect a child who is a ward of court. In practice, the court usually uses its powers under the Children Act 1989 (see above), apart from unusual circumstances such as restraining the publication of information which might be harmful to the ward. There is no power in wardship to make orders as between parents but the jurisdiction of the court under s 38 of the CCA and s 37 of the SCA can be invoked.

Damages claims

If parties are not married or cohabiting, an injunction can be granted within an action for damages for assault or trespass. Certain limitations are apparent. Harassment is not a tort as such but the courts are moving towards allowing a wider form of injunction in tort actions, relying on concepts of nuisance, etc. Injunctions have been granted in common law proceedings to prevent the making of persistent phone calls and to prevent a defendant from entering an 'exclusion zone'. However, in no circumstances can a power of arrest be attached to such an order. Also, pleadings are required and in theory the action could smoulder on, causing costs to accumulate.

Domestic Proceedings and Magistrates' Courts Act 1978

Applications to the magistrates' court under this Act can only be made by those who are married: s 16(1). Furthermore, the jurisdiction only covers assault, not harassment.

The orders available are:

(a) under s 16(2), that the respondent do not use or threaten to use violence against the person of the applicant or the child or both;

NOTES:

(b) under s 16(10), that the respondent do not incite or assist any other person so to use or threaten violence;

(c) under s 16(3), that the respondent be excluded from the matrimonial home.

The requirements for the grant of DPMCA orders are stringent. There will be an exclusion order only if the respondent has used violence against the applicant or a child of the family, or has threatened such violence and has used violence against another person, or has threatened violence against the applicant or the child in breach of a previous order. In addition, there must be a finding that the applicant or child is in danger of physical injury by the respondent.

Section 16(9) provides for expedited orders in cases of imminent danger. Evidence is given orally, not by affidavit, but there is provision for the filing of statements if required by the court.

Where an order is made, and there is a finding that the respondent has injured the applicant or a child of the family, and the court considers the respondent is likely to do it again, a power of arrest can be attached to the order, on similar principles to those governing powers of arrest under the DVMPA.

One advantage of using the magistrates' court jurisdiction is that depending on local listing it may be quicker than going to the county court.

Useful summaries of the relevant law are found in 'Family Courts: Emergency Remedies and Procedures', in Fricker, HHJ (ed), *Family Law*, 3rd edn, 1996, Jordan Publishing.

NOTES:

The application

Where?	Usually county court; sometimes High Court or magistrates' courts: see 'jurisdiction' above
Who?	County court – circuit/district judge High Court – High Court judge Magistrates' court – lay bench/stipendiary
Robes?	No, unless the claim is for common law injunction

Preliminaries

If the application is *ex parte*, be ready to explain to the court what the circumstances are justifying this, which must also be in the affidavit. If a power of arrest is sought, check that there is evidence to support the application. Under the DVMPA, there must be evidence, usually in the applicant's affidavit, of actual bodily harm, eg a bruise or a cut.

Whichever side you are on, always try to have a brief conference with your client beforehand. Find out what has happened, if anything, since the affidavit was sworn, and how the respondent reacted to service. Find out what alternative accommodation, if any, is available to each party. Make sure that your client understands the difference between undertakings and injunctions.

It may be possible to deal with other practicalities, for example, the mechanics of collecting personal belongings; which belongings; who is to be present. If parents are to be living apart for the first time, you may be able to agree on contact for the absent parent. In this way, the meeting at court can be a move towards reconciliation. But be careful: pushing hard on collateral issues can fan the flames!

At an *inter partes* hearing, very often the respondent is not represented (legal aid is not usually granted to resist a non-molestation application). See the section on litigants-in-

NOTES:

person in Chapter 2. If it is appropriate to speak to them at all (and you may encounter a great deal of hostility and mistrust), ask if they have seen a solicitor and find out what they know about undertakings. Offer to ask the judge to explain the implications so that they do not feel they have to take your word for it.

If the respondent is prepared to give an undertaking to the court, the terms of the undertaking can be identical to those of the order. Undertakings should be written out on standard forms, available from the court office. You should make sure that the respondent understands what might happen if the undertaking is breached, ie that one of the possible punishments is prison. Make sure also that the respondent is aware that the judge will warn him or her about that, but that this does not mean that the judge has made any findings about what has happened between the parties.

If the respondent is reluctant to give an undertaking, it sometimes helps to offer cross-undertakings. Whether you can advise the applicant to do this will depend on a number of factors, eg the respondent's mental state, the applicant's feelings about giving evidence, the risk of the court finding that the applicant has stirred up trouble for him or herself.

Hearing

This guide uses the example of an application under the DVMPA before a district judge in the county court.

Opening the case

In opening, the advocate should explain the nature of the application and its jurisdictional basis. If an agreement has been reached this should be explained to the court.

> *Madam, I appear for the applicant, my learned friend Mr Motorway represents the respondent. This is an application for non-molestation and ouster orders*

NOTES:

with power of arrest under the Domestic Violence and Matrimonial Proceedings Act 1976.

(If agreement has been reached, continue:)

I am glad to say that the parties have been able to reach an agreement in this matter, and the respondent is prepared to give an undertaking in the terms of the order sought. Madam, perhaps my learned friend and I could hand up the undertaking form.

(The district judge will read it, and then explain to the respondent the effect of the undertaking and ask if the respondent is willing to give the undertaking; she will then usually ask the respondent to sign the undertaking form. The advocate should then deal with costs: see below.)

(If there is no agreement, continue:)

This matter was last before the court a week ago, when District Judge Smith granted an ex parte order to last until today's date. There are affidavits from both parties. Have you had the opportunity to read these?

(If the answer is no:)

My client's affidavit was sworn on 26 December 1995. The opening paragraph explains that the parties have lived together for two years. The significant events are dealt with on the next page ...

(Take the district judge through the allegations on which the application is based, emphasising the most recent events, and pointing to evidence of actual bodily harm if a power of arrest is sought.)

You should also briefly summarise the respondent's affidavit. If it will require a more lengthy explanation you could invite your opponent to explain it to the judge.

NOTES:

Madam, you will see that the respondent filed an affidavit on 15 January 1996. From this you will see that the respondent denies that these incidents took place and is resisting the application. At paragraph 7, he also questions the court's power to hear this application under the DVMPA, arguing that the parties have never been married or cohabited as required by the Act. I understand that this argument is no longer proceeded with but perhaps my learned friend should explain the respondent's position on this point?

(If the answer is no:)

I'm grateful. Perhaps I could just point out ...

(Highlight most recent or most serious events, and actual bodily harm if required.)

Calling witnesses

If the evidence is contested it is very likely that the court will want to hear oral evidence from the parties.

Madam, unless you would like me to deal with any other points in opening, I call the applicant.

Begin by establishing the witness's identity as usual. Sometimes, applicants do not wish to disclose their address to the other party and the court should be told of this. Unless there is a reasonable objection, the witness will not be required to state an address in court but can confirm the address on the court file or write it down and hand it to the district judge. Ask the witness to identify the affidavit, take him or her through it briefly and ask him or her to deal with any new points not already included in the affidavit.

Call Janet Simpson.

(Witness will take the oath/affirm.)

NOTES:

Can you give the court your full name?

Madam, Miss Simpson has asked to be excused from disclosing her address and I understand my friend has no objection to that. Will you permit her simply to confirm that the address on the court file is still her current address?

(Obtain the witness's confirmation.)

Miss Simpson, you have sworn an affidavit in support of your application for non-molestation and ouster orders (Madam, the application is dated 26 December 1995, as is the affidavit). Can you look at this affidavit and confirm that is your signature at the end?

Take a look through it. Are all of its contents true, so far as you know?

(Take them through any parts that require clarification.)

Miss Simpson, at paragraph 5 of your affidavit you refer to an incident on 4 November, 1995 when you say the respondent caused you 'serious injuries', can you describe those injuries?

(Ask them to give evidence of any incidents not included in the affidavit.)

Miss Simpson, has Mr Brown been violent towards you since that time?

The witness will then be cross-examined by your opponent and the judge may have some questions.

Closing the case

In closing, applicants' advocates should review the evidence very briefly, highlighting details which make the case a serious one, and ensuring that jurisdictional requirements are satisfied. Advocates for both sides should be ready to deal with the question of the wider effect of granting/

NOTES:

refusing the order on the relationship, and on any children. Practicalities are also vital, for example, where an 'ousted' husband can live.

Costs

As in all family cases, the court is likely to be more ready to exercise its discretion to make no order as to costs, and this will be the usual order where the application is settled on undertakings. The effects of a costs order on the parties, their finances and any children, together with the incidence of legal aid, should all be taken into consideration.

What if ...?

The application is defective?

Sometimes the defect cannot be remedied, for example, where a cohabitee applies to magistrates under the DMPCA: this court has no jurisdiction to make an injunction regarding cohabitees (except possibly under the Children Act). In these circumstances, you must simply withdraw the application. If you could get to a county court within office hours, the applicant could issue an application and try to be heard *ex parte* under the DVMPA.

If the defect can be remedied by amendment, and the respondent is present, ask the court to allow the amendment without need to re-serve, on the grounds that the matter is urgent and the respondent has not been misled in any important respect.

If re-service is necessary and the case is urgent, ask for an order on an interim basis, *ex parte* if necessary and ask the court to abridge time for re-service if you think you can realistically get it done in less than the two days normally required. Also ask the court to fix a further hearing as soon as possible.

NOTES:

The applicant's affidavit is insufficient?

If there is no evidence of actual bodily harm although power of arrest has been sought, call the client, ask them to verify their affidavit, and then ask the judge's permission to adduce further evidence in chief. If it is granted, draw out the required evidence, for example:

> *When your husband hit you last Tuesday, what physical effect did it have on you?*

The applicant doesn't turn up?

See if you can find out what was the last contact with the applicant (eg when they last went to the solicitor's office). If you do not know why they are not there, ask the judge to read the affidavits. If the case is opposed or the judge is unwilling to make an order, seek to have the case adjourned to the earliest possible fixed date with costs reserved.

Your client turns violent?

For obvious reasons, many respondents in these cases are predisposed to violence but trouble can come from either side, particularly if other family members turn up to support the applicant. You must try to control your client, eg when waiting in the public areas of the court. If necessary, ask for help from court officials, though there is no guarantee that they will be able or willing to assist!

It is hard to reason with a distressed and angry client. Point out that by misbehaving he or she risks alienating the court and supporting the other side's case and that if it were to happen inside the court room it would be contempt.

Prevention is the best cure. It is important to get to court in good time so that a fight does not break out before you get there! Keep the parties as far apart as you can. If the weather

NOTES:

is fine, you could take your client outside. Always tell an usher if you are going far enough not to hear your case being called on. Make sure the parties do not leave the court at the same time and see whether the applicant needs to be accompanied anywhere.

You can only do your best. Although you should make every possible effort to keep trouble at bay, ultimately, you are responsible for the conduct of the case, not the conduct of your client.

Ancillary relief

The powers of the court to allocate resources between divorcing couples are very wide, and include the grant, declaration, variation or termination of the following: periodical payments for the benefit of one spouse or for the benefit of the children; rights of occupation of the matrimonial home; ownership of any matrimonial property and lump sum payments.

The orders themselves are frequently made by consent and the parties may make unlimited provision for each other, and attach any number of conditions. These may include undertakings by a party, for example, to be responsible for mortgage payments and other household outgoings, to pay off debts, or to do anything else which will assist in brokering a peace deal.

The court can make orders only where the jurisdictional requirements are satisfied: see *Jurisdiction* below. However, the parties are free to agree to whatever they like, and a court order can incorporate an undertaking by a party to do something which the court could not have ordered him to do.

NOTES:

The majority of such applications are resolved by consent even at the door of the court. Negotiation skills are often more important than advocacy. You still need complete command of the facts and figures of the case and the law involved. You must pay particular attention to costs and the effect of the Legal Aid Board's charge.

For a full picture of the law in this area we recommend: Duckworth, P, *Matrimonial Property and Finance*, 1995, FT Law and Tax (indispensable), and Jackson and Davies, *Matrimonial Finance and Taxation*, 5th edn, 1992, Butterworths.

You will also need to be armed with a certain amount of general knowledge about money, for example, tax rates, the effect of maintenance on entitlement to benefits, how to assess the value of a pension, government estimates of the cost of raising a child and any other factors relevant to the case you are doing. The publication *At a Glance*, published annually by the Family Law Bar Association, is a booklet which contains much of this information in table form and Street, M, *Money and Family Breakdown*, 2nd edn, 1994, Legal Action Group, is a very practical text. Also very useful (and extremely good value) are the Child Poverty Action Group's annual guides to different benefits.

Jurisdiction

Most of the court's powers on divorce are found in the Matrimonial Causes Act 1973. Sections 23 and 24 provide for a range of applications which can be made in a divorce petition or answer to a petition.

In addition, whether or not the parties are married (or divorced), Schedule 1 of the Children Act 1989 provides for wide-ranging financial relief for children.

NOTES:

Maintenance before divorce for a spouse or children is available under Part I of the Domestic Proceedings and Magistrates' Court Act 1978 (see *Which Court?* below).

Spouses' rights of occupation of their home are also subject to the Matrimonial Homes Act 1983, which provides that on the application of one spouse, another may have their rights of occupation terminated.

Section 30 of the Law of Property Act 1925 also provides that where there are co-owners of property, any owner may apply for an order that the property be sold (beware: reforms are forthcoming in this area; see ss 14 and 15 of the Trusts of Land and Appointment of Trustees Act 1996). The power to sell in divorce cases in found in s 24A of the MCA 1973, and in the High Court see RSC Order 31 r 1.

Maintenance for children is now principally assessed under the Child Support Act 1991 by the Child Support Agency. All applications made after 5 April 1993 will be dealt with the Agency, not the courts.

Only a limited number of applications can now be heard by the courts. For example, the court can make orders 'topping up' the Child Support assessment, deal with the obligations of step-parents, vary orders made before 5 April 1993 so long as the person with care is not in receipt of benefit or no CSA assessment has been carried out and make orders that a parent contribute to education costs. Once a maintenance assessment has been made, all court orders cease to have effect and the court has no power to vary them.

There is jurisdiction to make financial provision for children under both the Matrimonial Causes Act 1973 and under the Children Act 1989 but in both cases the jurisdiction is restricted by the Child Support Act.

NOTES:

The CSA decides the amount to be paid by applying a formula which has been much amended since the Act was originally passed. The court will want to know what the CSA calculation is going to be if the Agency have not yet made an assessment and even if it is not dealing with maintenance for children. This is a laborious calculation and requires a certain amount of information. However, it is an essential part of preparation for every case where there are children. Various computer programmes have been devised including *Child's Pay*, published by the Family Law Bar Association. It is also important to warn the client about the likely assessment and to explain that where the party with the child is in receipt of benefit, the Agency is obliged to make an assessment in respect of the absent parent.

In the family proceedings court, the Family Proceedings Courts (Children Act 1989) Rules 1991 and the Family Proceedings Courts (Matrimonial Proceedings) Rules 1991 govern procedure. In the other courts procedure is governed by the Family Proceedings Rules 1991.

Form of the application

The non-divorce based applications are self-explanatory. In a divorce, however, the petition must be carefully checked to see that there is an application for the precise form of relief required. If it is missing (eg one party requires an order for the sale of the matrimonial home, but has only payed periodical payments and lump sum relief), the petition must be amended. This is governed by the same rules as the amendment of any other pleading. If an amendment is sought on the day of the hearing, there is a strong likelihood of an adjournment, with the amending party penalised in costs, unless it is obvious from the correspondence what order is being sought.

NOTES:

The application

Where? County court/Family Division of the High Court (divorce-based applications), family proceedings court (applications under the Domestic Proceedings and Magistrates' Courts Act 1978); applications under the Children Act may be brought in any of these three forums

Who? County court – district judge/circuit judge
High Court – master/judge
Family proceedings court – lay bench

Robes? No

Preliminaries

Each party must produce affidavits of means (or in Children Act cases, statements under the Act). To these should be exhibited relevant documents to show the party's financial position, for example, bank and credit card statements, payslips, bills and correspondence. The court must be shown a clear view of what, precisely, each party possesses in terms of capital assets and net income and outgoings. In divorce cases where, until the hearing, everything is jointly owned, the emphasis is more on working out the value of the joint assets and pooled income, joint liabilities to be set against them, and practical ways in which the assets could be divided, together with a realistic view of what each party will need. Bear in mind the question of who will keep the children but also the needs of the absent parent with staying contact.

Never forget that the parties' liabilities will include their legal costs. You will need to know what the costs bill for each side will be, not forgetting that some costs will be incurred after the hearing. Where a party is legally aided and is not awarded costs, any property in the case which that party

NOTES:

recovers or preserves will be subject to a charge in favour of the Legal Aid Board for the amount of the costs, although the first £2,500 in family cases is exempt. The Board will not be fooled by any deals which give a party the benefit of property whilst trying to put it out of his possession and, therefore, out of reach of the charge. Even if such deals succeed in their aim, the Board may look to the party's advisers to repay the costs.

Where one party is awarded the matrimonial home, or money with which to buy a home, the Board's charge on this can be postponed. However, to secure this outcome, the court order must include certain 'magic words': see *Practice Direction* [1991] Fam Law 411.

Before the hearing you must prepare to cross-examine the other side on their affidavit(s)/statement(s). Carefully check all their figures. Are totals correct? Are the amounts of outgoings consistent with what you know of the person's lifestyle? Look out for double accounting: for example, in a list of outgoings, a party may have included an item for petrol, and another item for credit card bills. Checking carefully, you may find that all the petrol is bought with the credit card and the same item is being claimed twice. Ask yourself whether the outgoings include extravagant or unnecessary items, or whether any potential source of income is being neglected. Check bank statements to be sure that most of the income and outgoings are passing through the account. The person may secretly have another account.

What use you make of all this information depends on what your client wants. If you have no clear instructions on how your client wishes property to be divided, try to find your own solution, ie an arrangement which will provide for any children, allow both parties a standard of living as close as possible to that which they previously enjoyed, and which

NOTES:

will take account of costs. With the help of textbooks explore common solutions. Often the asset position will dictate the primary solution which frequently remains that the house will go with the children to the mother.

If you know what your client wants, ask yourself if it is realistic, and what concessions might be offered to the other side in return for it. Be ready to explain the feasibility of any proposed outcome to your client. There is no point in asking the court to do the impossible, and proposing the impossible in negotiation will only alienate the other side.

In certain specified courts, a new procedure applies to applications for ancillary relief begun after 1 October 1996. See *Practice Direction: Ancillary Relief Procedure: Pilot Scheme* [1996] 2 FLR 368.

Hearing

Orders by consent

Very often, the hearing is a two-minute affair, approving a consent order after hours of negotiation.

The negotiation itself, however, is a delicate business. You must always have a clear idea of the scope of your instructions. If your client will never accept a particular deal, do not waste time with your opponent suggesting or discussing it. In negotiating, make sure your opponent understands the basis on which you are talking. If you are revealing some fact 'between counsel', ie for the ears of no one else, say so. The approach of advocates varies widely. There are some cases where a relatively confrontational style is necessary, perhaps in order to see off unrealistic suggestions which the other side is obstinate in making, but these are rare. Where the parties are at war, a reasonable outcome is likely to be facilitated if the advocates can maintain polite and frank communication.

NOTES:

The negotiations may be lengthy. Keep the usher and the judge informed and ask for more time. You may have to go and see the judge, which might actually help things along (see *What if ...?* below). Do not let yourself be hurried, particularly at the drafting stage.

The end product of a successful negotiation is a consent order. If there is time, write it out in full so that you can hand it up to the judge. If the order involves one party giving undertakings to the court, it should (in the county court) be written on an 'undertakings form', available from the court office. It does not matter which advocate writes out the order, but both should carefully check that it contains exactly what the parties have agreed. Familiarise yourself with precedents for such orders: there are many virtually standard provisions for stock situations and you should take copies to court. There are some in Duckworth, *Precedents for Consent Orders*, Vol 2, 4th edn, 1995, Solicitors Family Law Association, which is excellent.

Many divorce settlements are on a 'clean break' basis, ie finally dismissing all parties' applications for ancillary relief; others are 'until further order', so that the case can be re-opened if the parties' circumstances change. Remember that even in 'clean break' cases, there is no such thing as a clean break so far as children are concerned.

The order should always be read back and explained to the client and, once approved, be signed by both sides or their advocates before going to the judge.

When you go into court with a consent order, the party whose application it is should rise and say (the examples in this chapter illustrate an application in a divorce case in the county court before a circuit judge).

NOTES:

May it please your Honour, I represent the petitioner and my learned friend Miss Bloggins represents the respondent. This is my client's application for final (or interim) ancillary relief. I am pleased to say that the parties have come to an agreement, and my learned friend and I have prepared a draft consent order. May I hand it up?

This may be all that either advocate has to say, though the judge may ask you questions about the order or suggest changes. Since the order is expressed as a consent order, your client must agree to any changes and you should ask for time to take instructions. If the client does not agree, a full hearing may be necessary. If you are against a litigant-in-person, be ready to do more explaining to the judge, who will want to be sure that no advantage has been taken of the other side.

It is considered polite to leave a gap in the draft order for a certificate for counsel, rather than just awarding this to yourself. But, if the judge does not then suggest the certificate, you must of course ask for it.

Contested hearings

As in any other trial, you must concentrate on what the real issues are and on what remedy your client seeks. It is important to remember to base your presentation of the case on the real issues, because the parties will often try to use their affidavits or court appearance simply to air grievances against each other. It is up to you to keep your side of the hearing under control.

The party whose application it is will generally open the case in the usual way. Tell the judge the basic facts and refer him to the written evidence. If you have a particular outcome in mind, now is the time to air it.

NOTES:

May it please your Honour, I appear for the petitioner, Mrs Smith, and my learned friend Miss Bloggins appears for the respondent, Mr Smith. This is the hearing of the petitioner's application for final ancillary relief. Has your Honour had a chance to look through the papers?

(If not, continue:)

The parties were married on 4 December 1980. Decree nisi was on 10 January 1993 and was made absolute on 5 May 1993. There are three children of the family: Joanne, aged 5; David, aged 3 and Dana, aged 18 months. There is a residence order in favour of the mother, and the father has staying contact with the two elder children each weekend.

Your Honour will see that each party has sworn two affidavits. Perhaps I should pause here and let your Honour look through those.

(Usually, the judge will now read the affidavits, though he or she may ask you to summarise them or to direct him to the relevant parts. Alternatively, he or she may suggest that these should wait until each party comes to give evidence.)

Following the above, or immediately if the judge has read the papers, go onto the question of the assets, but be fairly brief.

Your Honour will see that there is equity in the matrimonial home of some £10,000, and also that on the respondent's own case, he has disposable income over and above his housing and basic needs of £50 per week. Your Honour, the order I shall be seeking today is that the matrimonial home be transferred into the petitioner's name. With your Honour's permission, I call the petitioner.

The witness takes the oath and gives name and address as usual. Then you ask:

NOTES:

Mrs Smith, did you swear an affidavit (or sign a statement) on 10 November 1995` Is this the affidavit you swore? Is there anything in the affidavit that you wish to change or correct?

With the judge's permission, you may now examine-in-chief on any peripheral matters or new information which has arisen since the affidavit was sworn. Otherwise, simply say:

Just wait there please.

At this point in the other side's evidence, you may now cross-examine. Resist any pressure you may be under from your client to cross-examine on irrelevant issues. Past details of the other party's behaviour are very seldom helpful in determining how the property should be shared out. Focus on the figures. Highlight any falsehood or exaggeration. Your case will be strengthened if you can show that your client's figures are more reliable than the other side's. Probe the other party's needs and, if the solution you want would work better than what the other party suggests, try to make him or her admit this. Where a party is placing his or her interests above those of the children of the family, capital can be made of this. If he or she is saying that cheaper properties are available, ask what is known about them, whether he or she has visited them, what sort of area they are in, are they convenient for schools, etc. You must strike a balance between being thorough and searching on the one hand, and pedantic on the other. Where there are clear points which you can score in cross-examination, do not bury these beneath dozens more questions which may not get you anywhere.

After the evidence has been heard, there are closing speeches from the party making the application and then from the other side. Succinctly suggest the solution which you would like the court to adopt, and take the judge to the

NOTES:

figures which support such a solution. You may cite any rules of law which are applicable, though this is often not necessary. A great deal of the case law in this area simply attempts to embody common sense and the court is unlikely to need reminding of it. However, where a point of principle arises, for example, as to how to proceed in a particular situation, and there is a case directly on the point, briefly draw the judge's attention to it and to any open offers which have been made.

After the judgment you must deal with costs. Again, law is unlikely to be helpful. The usual order is that costs follow the event as in all other cases, but in a family case, especially where one party is legally aided, the court is more likely to be receptive to an application for no order. You will do better to concentrate on the facts, pointing out to the judge what costs order will cause least hardship or that both parties have contributed to unnecessary costs being incurred.

What if ...?

The hearing date arrives and one party has still not produced an affidavit/statement?

In practice, you cannot go ahead with a contested hearing in these circumstances. However, if information is forthcoming on the defaulting party's means and the other party is willing to rely on that information, there is nothing to stop you seeking a negotiated settlement. If you represent the other party you should explain the risks of going ahead without confirmed information. Otherwise, the matter will have to be adjourned with a direction that the defaulting party file an affidavit or statement within a specified time. In the case of persistent default this order can have a penal notice attached to it. If you do agree a consent order, the other party's representative will probably have to reassure

NOTES:

the judge that his or her client is justified in relying on the information provided at court.

In conference you discover that some of the contents of your client's affidavit/statement are untrue?

You must not connive in presenting an untrue account to the court. You have a duty not to mislead the court and the client has a continuing duty of full and frank disclosure. Moreover, if the untruth is discovered, your client's credibility will fall apart. In the case of a small discrepancy, have your client make the alteration themselves and show a copy of the altered version to the other side. If the document is an affidavit, the corrected version must forthwith be re-sworn (ask at the court office). You will have to explain this turn of events to the court or your opponent as best you can. If there is not time to do this, deal with it in examination-in-chief.

If the discrepancy is serious, there are two options. The first is to make a clean breast of it in court. Deal with it during your client's evidence-in-chief so as to take some of the sting out of the cross-examination which will follow. Alternatively, if you think your client could undo some of the damage with more time to reflect, you could tell the other side and the court that your client has become confused about his or her evidence and needs to produce a new affidavit/statement. Ask for an adjournment. You may be refused and, even if the adjournment is granted, expect costs to be awarded against your client.

The client wants to give up and submit to an unfavourable settlement?

These cases are emotionally wearing, and clients regularly become dispirited and give up hope. If your client orders you to settle the case on unfavourable terms, then ultimately you must do so. However, you should resist this. If you

NOTES:

think that your client's emotions are preventing him or her from giving properly considered instructions, then you should discontinue any negotiation. The client in such a situation will not want to press ahead with a hearing but, if he or she can be persuaded to do so, his or her documentary evidence will go before the judge, who may impose a better outcome than you could achieve by negotiation in such a situation. If you are instructed to settle the case on an unfavourable basis and if someone else is with you, make sure that the other person takes an independent note of what happens and of what advice you have given. If you are on your own make a written note and ask the client to sign it.

You believe that your opponent is playing for time?

Negotiations in these cases can be extremely protracted. The court list can be very crowded. If the negotiations break down, it may be impossible to hear the case that day and sometimes opponents try to spin out negotiations precisely because of this. This may prolong the suffering for an impecunious party or put pressure on a party because of the further costs to be incurred.

If there is a risk of running out of time, impose an ultimatum. Tell the other side that you will not shift far from your current negotiating position, and that if there is no sensible offer by a certain time, the case will have to be contested. The second step is to carry out that threat if there has been no improvement.

An alternative (or supplementary) solution is to tell the other side that if there is no time for a final hearing, you will ask the court to make an interim order, for example, for one party to pay maintenance. When you go into court, state the position in your opening speech:

Notes:

This is my client's application ... (as above). The parties have been talking but unfortunately have been unable to reach an agreement. Your Honour will realise that there is now insufficient time to conclude a full hearing today. However, I should like to ask the court to make an interim order (for periodical payments, etc as appropriate) on the basis of the affidavit evidence.

The threat of taking this course may have some effect. However, remember that the court is unlikely to make such an order unless a fairly clear case can be made on the basis of both parties' affidavits/statements.

Children Act applications

Applications relating to children fall mainly under the Children Act 1989 which came into force in October 1991. The 1989 Act deals with the issues of care and supervision by local authorities (public law applications) as well as the issues of residence and contact between parents and guardians (private law applications). The paramount principle to be applied by any court when considering any question with respect to the upbringing of a child or a child's property is the welfare of the child. A child is anybody under the age of 18 but care or supervision orders cannot be made when a child is over 17 and s 8 orders which affect children over the age of 16 will only be made in exceptional circumstances. The court has to have regard to the welfare checklist set out in s 1.

The main regulations to which you will need to refer are the Family Proceedings Rules 1991 and the Family Proceedings Courts (Children Act 1989) Rules 1991.

This chapter deals first with private law applications and then with public law applications. Whichever you are

NOTES:

dealing with, and particularly in the family proceedings court, it may be useful to structure your submissions around the headings of a pro forma 'reasons' form which has been developed for use in that court, which include the following:

(a) facts agreed or not in dispute;

(b) facts in dispute;

(c) findings of fact;

(d) the extent to which witnesses were believed or disbelieved and the information on which the court relied in reaching its decision;

(e) cases considered;

(f) whether a welfare report was considered (and how it influenced the court);

(g) the welfare checklist.

Private law orders

The principal orders the court can make under this Act are to be found at s 8. There are four types of 's 8 order':

(a) Contact order. An order requiring the person with whom the child is living to allow the child to visit or stay or otherwise have contact with the person named in the order;

(b) Prohibited steps order. An order that no specified step which could be taken by a person in meeting his parental responsibility for a child shall be taken without the consent of the court;

(c) Residence order. An order settling the arrangements to be made as to the person with whom a child is to live;

(d) Specific issue order. An order giving directions for the purpose of determining a question which has arisen in

NOTES:

connection with any aspect of parental responsibility for a child.

The 1989 Act sets out those who may apply for these orders as of right; everyone else has to get leave before issuing an application. A person who is entitled to make an application or any other person with leave can apply for an order in any 'family proceedings' in which a question arises with respect to the welfare of a child. 'Family proceedings' are proceedings under any of the enactments listed in s 8(4). The court can also make s 8 orders of its own motion in family proceedings.

There are various restrictions on making s 8 orders: these are set out in s 9. For example, the court cannot make a residence order in favour of a local authority.

It is a principle of the Act (s 1(5)) that the court shall not make any order unless it considers that doing so would be better for the child than not making an order. It is for the applicant to show that it is in the child's interest that the court should make an order. This will not be difficult where there is a dispute between the parties on a specific issue, but sometimes after the parents have reached an agreement one parent seeks to 'formalise' the position by obtaining a court order. Where there is a clear agreement, an order will not usually be made unless, for example, it is necessary because of past disagreements or to make the child feel more secure or there is a risk of abduction.

Factors that are relevant when the court is considering the child's welfare are listed in s 3 and include the wishes and feelings of the child, his or her physical, emotional and educational needs and how capable each of his or her parents, or other relevant person, is of meeting his or her needs.

NOTES:

Another order an unmarried father may apply for is a parental responsibility order under s 4. 'Parental responsibility' means all the rights, duties, powers, responsibilities and authority which by law a parent of a child has in relation to the child and his property (s 3(1)). Where the child's parents were married at the time of the child's birth, each parent will have parental responsibility. Where they were not married, only the mother automatically has parental responsibility. The father can acquire parental responsibility by obtaining a court order or if both parents agree to provide for the father to have parental responsibility. A 'parental responsibility agreement' must be in a prescribed form.

An application under the Act is usually made on a particular form in which there will be a paragraph requiring the applicant to set out why he or she is seeking an order. The respondent is supposed to file an answer setting out his or her views on the application.

Ex parte applications can be made for s 8 orders but they will normally only be appropriate when there is an urgent need for an order, for example, when there is a risk of abduction or violence.

Once the application has been made, parties are usually encouraged to attend a conciliation appointment. This is a meeting between the parties and a trained conciliator, for the purpose of attempting to resolve the dispute without a trial. The procedure regarding conciliation varies from court to court but usually, once an application is issued, the court will fix a date. If at the conciliation appointment it becomes clear that the dispute cannot be resolved by agreement, a directions appointment will be fixed. Sometimes these are listed back to back with the conciliation appointment and

NOTES:

some courts require representatives to attend (you may need to draft an order if agreement is reached).

Directions should set the timetable for the case and could include dates for exchange of statements if this has not already been done, preparation of a welfare officer's or local authority report, exchange of any reports or documents, etc. Some courts have standard directions. In the family proceedings court, directions may be made by a clerk without the involvement of the magistrates.

At the directions stage or earlier, either party can apply for a so-called 'interim' order, ie an order which lasts for a temporary period or until the final hearing (s 11(3)). It is fairly common for an interim order for contact to be made to see how it goes. A change of residence is much less likely to be ordered before the full hearing.

Many courts have adopted the practice of fixing a final directions hearing shortly before the full hearing so that the trial judge can review the state of the case, check that all previous directions have been complied with, whether the case can be compromised or whether the issues can be narrowed.

One of the most useful books to take to court with you is White, Carr and Lowe, *The Children Act in Practice*, 2nd edn, 1995, Butterworths. The updated work, McFarlane, H, 'Children Law and Practice', in *Family Law*, Jordan Publishing is also excellent.

The application

Where?	High Court, county court, family proceedings court
Who?	High Court – High Court judge County court – circuit judge

NOTES:

Family proceedings court – magistrates
See the Children (Allocation of Proceedings) Order 1991.

Robes? No

Preliminaries

Children Act matters are heard in chambers and usually take priority over the rest of the day's list. You should attend court with enough time to allow you to meet your client and your opponent as there are often new developments or settlement proposals in these cases. If there is a welfare officer, confirm with your opponent that there is no objection to your discussing the case with the welfare officer, or talk to them together. If there are any new developments or settlement proposals discuss them with the welfare officer.

Find out and discuss with your opponent whether there is a suitable neutral third party who might be prepared to supervise contact such as grandmother, uncle or aunt. Make sure you know whether they agree to do so and what time they will be available.

If you are considering a settlement involving contact at a family centre (not the same thing as supervised contact), find out about the availability of local contact centres, particularly their referral criteria, waiting list and opening hours. The court office may be able to provide contact numbers.

Hearing

The applicant's advocate should introduce the parties, the application and any papers:

> *May it please your Honour, I appear for the applicant mother, Mrs White. Mrs Jones who sits to my left appears for the respondent father, Mr White. Your Honour, the mother's application is for a residence*

NOTES:

order in respect of Kelly White who was born on 25 September 1990. The father opposes the application and has made a cross application for residence. The mother's application is dated 23 October 1995 and her statement dated 1 November should be before your Honour, as should be father's answer and statement dated 7 November 1995. A welfare officer's report has been prepared by a Mrs James who is also in court today. I believe your Honour should also have an agreed bundle of documents prepared by the applicant dealing with Kelly's schooling.

Then, briefly, go through the history of the case:

The parents were married for five years from 1990 to 1995. They separated in June 1995 but are not yet divorced, though Mrs White filed a petition earlier this year. Kelly was born on 25 September 1990 and is now six years old. She lived with her father immediately after the separation but went to live with her mother in the summer of 1995. There was a conciliation appointment on 1 December but no agreement was reached. Directions were given by District Judge Jefferies on 3 January ordering that a welfare report be filed and that the welfare officer should attend today's hearing, and fixing the final hearing for today.

It has been said that there is a 'spectrum of procedure in family cases from the *ex parte* application on minimal evidence to the full and detailed investigations on oral evidence which may be prolonged' (Butler Sloss LJ, *Re B (Minors) (Contact)* [1994] 2 FLR 1 at 5). The case gives some guidelines on the approach to be adopted by the judge in considering what evidence to hear. Tell the judge what you are proposing to do about evidence and check whether he or she agrees. If oral evidence is heard, the welfare officer usually goes first and their evidence may be decisive. When

NOTES:

you get to your witnesses, begin by simply asking them to confirm the contents of the statement:

I call Mrs White.
Can you give the court your full name and address?
What is your occupation?
If you look at the last page of the document in front of you dated 1 November 1995, is that your signature?
Have you read that statement through recently?
Can you confirm that the contents of that statement are true to the best of your knowledge and belief?
Mrs White, has anything happened since that date that is relevant in helping the court decide who Kelly should live with?

Then go through the contested parts of the answer and statement filed by the respondent:

Mrs White, at paragraph 3 of his statement Mr White states that he has always been a loving and caring father, do you agree with him? ...
Mr White suggests that if Kelly were to live with him, her schooling would not be affected. Can you begin by telling the court, to the best of your knowledge, how much involvement he has had with Kelly's schooling?
Has he attended any of the parents' meetings?
Did he assist in choosing this school for Kelly?
Has he ever taken Kelly to school?
Mrs White we see from the reports that initially Kelly had a few difficulties at school. Were you ever advised of the cause of those problems?
How is she doing now?
If she were to go and live with Mr White would you regard it as being in her best interests to carry on attending this school?
How far is Mr White's new property from the school?
What time does school start?
How long would it take to drive to the school in the

NOTES:

morning from Mr White's house?
When must Kelly be collected by? ...

Conclude by asking the witness to remain in the box for cross-examination:

Thank you, would you wait there. My friend may have some questions.

If the matter can be dealt with by submissions alone then these should be logical and avoid unnecessary criticisms of the other party.

(Submissions for the respondent:)

Your Honour has read the various statements and documents in this case. I do not propose to go through them in any detail save to say that in my submission there are three clear and convincing arguments as to why the mother's application for a residence order should fail and why the father should be granted a residence order in respect of Kelly:

(a) The mother is under severe financial pressure at the moment and seems unlikely to be able to extricate herself from these problems in the near future. An agreement in respect of the finances was reached after separation and Mr White has kept up his maintenance payments but Mrs White has lost a great deal of money in her risky business ventures. Meanwhile, Kelly is suffering, not only because she is having to do without the items that the rest of her schoolmates have, but also because she bears the brunt of her mother's anxiety over her financial troubles. Consequently, as the welfare officer points out at page 17 of her report, Kelly does not get the attention she needs;

(b) The father has settled down with his new girl-friend in their modest but comfortable property. Kelly gets on well with Miss Simons and enjoys staying with

Notes:

her father and his girlfriend. At her age, Kelly desperately needs some stability and security. She needs to feel she is part of a family unit and this is the feeling she has when she is with Mr White and Miss Simons;

(c) Kelly has had educational difficulties in the past and, whilst it is accepted that she is doing better now, it is submitted that her present school does not have the facilities to give her the additional help she needs. Your Honour has seen the reports on the school Mr White proposes to send her to, and Your Honour will have noted that it is not possible for Mrs White to send Kelly there as she is outside the catchment area. This is a splendid school with a proven record of assisting young children with difficulties such as Kelly's. The headmaster has stated in his letter that he would be prepared to offer Kelly a place if she can enrol before the start of the new term.

Depending on the facts of the particular case, it may be advisable to ask the court to make an order which goes into details about hours of contact, date for transfer of residence, etc. Alternatively, the court may just make an order for reasonable contact, leaving the parties to work out the details between them. Either way, the court is likely to want to know what the practical arrangements are going to be so make sure you have thought about the following:

(a) commencement date and time of contact;

(b) duration;

(c) location;

(d) collection and return;

(e) supervision (if any);

(f) prohibitions (if any), for example, no contact with a specified third party.

NOTES:

The court may announce its decision immediately or it may be reserved, depending on the complexity of the case. The family proceedings courts have to give reasons for their decision and often provide these in writing, although not necessarily immediately. It is worth checking whether they are going to send on a copy so that you know whether you need to take a full note.

At the end of the proceedings in the county court/High Court, do not forget to ask for legal aid taxation and certificate(s) for counsel, if appropriate. It is not necessary to do this in the family proceedings court, as authority to instruct counsel should be obtained in advance of the hearing.

What if ...?

The judge wishes to hear from the child in question?

Unless the child is a party to the proceedings, he or she should not really be at court at all. Even if the child is a party, the court may exclude them from the hearing if they are represented. However, if child minders cannot be found, it is sometimes unavoidable for the children to be present outside court.

In some, fairly rare, circumstances and where the child is sufficiently mature (at least five years old, and probably a lot older) to be asked a few questions, the judge may decide to speak to them. The advocate might suggest that the court considers seeing the child or, more usually, the court itself will suggest it. If you think it might be a good idea for the court to do this, discuss it with the other advocates and, in particular, the court welfare officer or guardian *ad litem*. You will have to be prepared to give an extremely good reason where there is already a CWO or GAL involved. It may be that the child will ask to see the judge.

NOTES:

Usually, the court will see the child in private, although the conversation cannot be confidential, if relevant matters materialise. It is very rare for a child to be asked questions in the witness box but it does happen, especially with older children. Equally, the older child may be allowed to sit in court and listen to the proceedings, if the court thinks this appropriate.

You have agreed an order?

Often matters are compromised in the court corridor. If so, a consent order should be drawn up covering all issues. The advocate representing the applicant should briefly introduce the parties and, if the court has been kept waiting whilst you were negotiating, it is always polite to apologise for the delay and to thank the judge for his or her patience. Then give a brief background to the case and ask the judge if he or she has had an opportunity to read the papers. If so, you can inform him that the matter has been settled and a draft order has been drawn up. Hand up the written order and explain any unusual or complicated parts. The judge will read the order and may propose some amendments or have a few questions. Be prepared to explain the reasoning behind the agreement. A judge may be reluctant to make any order bearing in mind the principle of 'no order unless necessary'. You should be ready to substantiate the need for any order in your case, for example, that the parties have been unable to stick to informal agreements in the past.

Care proceedings

The Children Act 1989 also imposes on local authorities various duties in relation to children which include safeguarding and promoting the welfare of children and (so far as is consistent with that duty) promoting the upbringing of such children by their families, and providing accommodation for children in need in certain circumstances.

NOTES:

There are a large number of different applications and orders which may be made in relation to children under the Children Act 1989. The following is an outline of the most common orders in respect of which applications are made:

(a) care order (or interim care order) (s 31);

(b) supervision order (or interim supervision order) (s 31) including an education supervision order (s 36);

(c) child assessment order (s 43);

(d) emergency protection order (s 44).

Care order or Supervision order

Such an order may be made if:

(a) the child concerned is suffering, or is likely to suffer, significant harm; *and*

(b) the harm or likelihood of harm is attributable to;

  (i) the care given to the child, or likely to be given to him if the order were not made, not being what it would be reasonable to expect a parent to give to him; or

  (ii) the child's being beyond parental control.

On hearing an application for either a care order or a supervision order, the court make may either order, ie not necessarily the order applied for (s 31(5)) and may make other orders including orders for parental responsibility and contact orders under s 34.

Applications for care or supervision orders may be made by either a local authority or an 'authorised person' (ie the NSPCC or a person authorised by the Secretary of State).

In deciding whether harm is significant, the child's health and development should be compared with the health and

NOTES:

development which could reasonably be expected of a similar child (s 31(10)).

Before making a care order the court *'shall'*:

(a) consider the arrangements which the authority have made, or propose to make, for affording any person contact with a child (ie parent, guardian, person in whose favour a residence order was made, or someone having care of the child by order under the inherent jurisdiction of the High Court); and

(b) invite the parties to the proceedings to comment on those arrangements (s 34(11)).

The effect of a care order is that (s 33):

(a) the local authority receives the child into its care and keeps the child in its care for the duration of the order;

(b) the local authority obtains parental responsibility for the child;

(c) the local authority may determine the extent to which a parent or guardian of the child may meet his parental responsibility for him (if the local authority is satisfied that it is necessary to do so in order to safeguard or promote the child's welfare).

The effect of a supervision order (s 35) is that the supervisor is under a duty:

(a) to advise, assist and befriend the supervised child;

(b) to take such steps as are reasonably necessary to give effect to the order;

(c) to consider whether or not to vary or discharge the order if:

    (i) the order is not wholly complied with; or

NOTES:

(ii) the supervisor considers that the order may no longer be necessary.

Powers of court

Section 37(1):

> Where in any family proceedings in which a question arises with respect to the welfare of any child, it appears to the Court that it may be appropriate for a care or supervision order to be made with respect to him, the court may direct the appropriate authority to undertake an investigation into the child's circumstances.

In which event, the local authority *shall* consider whether they should:

(a) apply for a care order or a supervision order with respect to the child;

(b) provide services or assistance for the child or his family; or

(c) take any other action with respect to the child.

The local authority is under a duty to investigate within eight weeks and to report to the court if no application for a care order or supervision order is to be made. See the Best Practice Guidance on s 37 Directions in the *Children Act Annual Report* 1992/3, Annex 1, p 40.

Interim orders

If there is an application for an adjournment in an application for a care or supervision order, or if the court directs a s 37 investigation, the court may make an interim care order or an interim supervision order (see the case of *Hampshire County Council v S* [1993] Fam 158), if the court is satisfied that there are reasonable grounds for considering that the criteria for a care order or supervision order (see above) are met. The first interim order can only last eight weeks, but

NOTES:

after that interim orders can only be made for four week periods. Sometimes, the court will be prepared to make interim orders by consent with either the local authority or no one at all attending but a specific direction must be sought authorising this.

When making an interim care order or an interim supervision order, the court may make any directions that it considers appropriate with regard to the medical or psychiatric examination or other assessment of the child.

The application

Where?	High Court/county court/family proceedings court
Who?	High Court – High Court judge County court – circuit judge Family proceedings court – lay bench See the Children (Allocation of Proceedings) Order 1991
Robes?	No

Preliminaries

Care proceedings are usually begun in the family proceedings court (unless they are brought as a result of a s 37 report or there are pending proceedings elsewhere or the application is to extend, vary or discharge an order made in another court) but they may be transferred up in certain circumstances. See the Children (Allocation of Proceedings) Order 1991.

Care proceedings tend to be fairly lengthy, even at the directions stage, with a number of advocates, experts, social workers, guardians *ad litem*, parents and members of the extended family and sometimes foster carers involved.

NOTES:

For this reason, it is important to heed the warning of the High Court that directions appointments should not be treated as formalities. A high level of co-operation between the parties' representatives is required to ensure that the case is managed properly. There are a number of reported cases and practice directions on this subject and space does not allow them to be considered fully here. However, matters which should be discussed between the parties and agreed if possible include time estimates (not forgetting reading time, time for opening and closing submissions and time for the examination and cross-examination of each witness by each party), the disclosure of papers to witnesses, the obtaining of all relevant material from its various sources, the co-ordination of experts (by a meeting of experts, if this will save time and clarify issues), preparation of court bundles, chronologies and skeleton arguments.

The court will expect you to avoid an aggressive style of cross-examination wherever possible, bearing in mind that the parties have to continue their relationship once the court case is over. That said, it is obviously your duty to put your client's case as forcefully and effectively as possible. It is a difficult balance.

Hearing

The local authority will make its application by introducing the legal representatives of those in court:

> *May it please your Honour, I appear on behalf of the Blackshire local authority and make an application for a care order in respect of Amber and Scarlet Rose. My learned friend Mr Green appears on behalf of the mother, Violet Rose, Mrs Red appears on behalf of the father, Brian Rose, Miss Yellow appears on behalf of the maternal grandmother who was given leave to intervene by His Honour Judge Pink on 22 April 1994*

NOTES:

and Mrs Magenta appears on behalf of the guardian ad litem, *Mrs White.*

I am hopeful that your Honour has had an opportunity of reading the papers/bundle.

There is quite likely to be a large bundle of documents. Although judges are supposed to have read the papers, they will not always have been able to in which case you may have to adjourn for the judge to do so, directing them to the relevant documents in the bundle if the issues have narrowed as they often do at the door of the court. Once they have been read, it is usually appropriate to keep the opening short, especially if skeleton arguments have been made.

Briefly go through the history of the case with reference to the chronology identifying any disputed incidents:

The mother and father started living together in 1985 and married in June 1987 just before Amber Rose was born on 7 July 1987. Amber is now six years old. The local authority have been involved with the family since that time. Amber was placed on the Child Protection Register in September 1988 following a non-accidental injury to her head. On 18 November 1989 Scarlet Rose was born ...

End the opening by spelling out the significant harm relied on and the findings sought, summarising the local authority's care plan and the attitude of each party to it.

Then call your evidence. The legal representatives cross-examine in the following order: parties with parental responsibility, other respondents and finally the guardian *ad litem*.

May I call Mrs Grey.
Please state your full name, occupation and professional address.

NOTES:

What are your qualifications?
What is your experience/How long have you been a social worker?
Did you prepare and sign the statements dated 3 June 1994 and 8 August 1994 which are found on pages 36 and 89 of the bundle in front of you?
Can you confirm that the contents of those statements are true to the best of your knowledge and belief?

Ask any questions to bring the court up-to-date or to expand on areas of the care plan, as necessary.

Conclude by asking the witness to remain in the box for further questioning:

Thank you, would you just wait there.

After the evidence has been heard, and when summing up, bear in mind the appropriate criteria. If your submissions are identical to those already put forward by another legal representative, do not be afraid to adopt the submissions and sit down quickly. Closing speeches usually follow this order: respondents without parental responsibility, parties with parental responsibility, applicant, guardian *ad litem*.

What if ...?

The father and mother decide at court that they would like to be separately represented because there is a conflict of interest?

There is very little else that can be done except to ask the court to adjourn the proceedings. You will have to explain to the court what the difficulty is about joint representation and why this was not apparent before.

A family member wishes to intervene at the hearing?

Leave will have to be obtained from the judge to intervene explaining the intervenor's interest in the proceedings and

NOTES:

why it is necessary for him to intervene. If leave is granted, all parties should consider whether an adjournment is necessary.

There are criminal proceedings pending?

The fact that there are criminal proceedings is not necessarily a reason to adjourn the care proceedings, nor can a party get out of giving evidence for fear of self-incrimination. Only evidence concerning child abduction is protected and then only in respect of statements made outside court. The court has to consider whether it is in the interests of the child for the Children Act case to be delayed. One of the factors to be taken into account is the effect on the parent's ability to participate in the care proceedings (both in terms of giving evidence and in terms of the effect on the care proceedings if the parent were to get a custodial sentence) but it is not determinative. It will be important to look at the interrelationship between the criminal charge and the allegations on which the local authority case is based. If the criminal charge is murder, the care proceedings are highly likely to be adjourned. There are a number of reported decisions to which reference should be made; including *Re TB (Care Proceedings: Criminal Trial)* [1995] 2 FLR 801.

You need to get evidence from a third party?

There is *obiter* authority for the proposition that discovery from a third party can be ordered in both private and public law Children Act applications (*Re A & B (Minors) (No 2)* [1995] 1 FLR 351). However, the safest and least controversial option is to issue a witness summons against the third party under CCR Order 20 r 12 (RSC Order 38 r 14).

The parents consent to a care or supervision order?

As with any other consent order, you may need to draft the terms of the order particularly where specific contact is

NOTES:

agreed and to deal with the conditions to be attached to the supervision order. It is also helpful to draft out agreed facts and so on as suggested at the beginning of this section. Whichever party you represent, you need to think through the factual basis on which the court will be invited to find that the threshold criteria have been made out. Some concession will be needed from the parents as to abuse or neglect, etc but the court will not want to go into narrow differences of wording. If you cannot agree or the court is not satisfied by the concessions made, there may have to be oral evidence limited to the major facts which establish the criteria.

NOTES:

6 : Contempt of court

There are two types of contempt of court:

(a) criminal contempt: words or acts obstructing, or tending to obstruct or interfere with, the administration of justice;

(b) civil contempt: failure or neglect to comply with an order of or undertaking to the court.

This chapter is only concerned with the second type.

Civil contempt

An application to commit for contempt is an application to enforce an order made by, or an undertaking made to, the court.

The procedural rules must be followed to the letter. As the application necessarily involves an allegation that a court order or an undertaking to the court has been breached, and because the respondent's liberty is potentially at risk, such applications are treated particularly seriously by the courts.

Such applications are quasi-criminal and the applicant must prove his case to the criminal standard: 'beyond any reasonable doubt'. Hearsay evidence is not admissible.

Most committal applications dealt with by the junior advocate will be made in the county court under Order 29. If a defendant is arrested under a power of arrest, the police will notify the applicant so that an application for committal can be made to the court as a matter of urgency. The court can proceed without a formal application having been drawn up and served, but it will do so only in exceptional circumstances and will almost always want to know the

NOTES:

applicant's views as to punishment. A defendant cannot be remanded in custody so he would have to be released pending any adjourned hearing.

The applicant must ensure, and be able to prove, that:

(a) An order or undertaking was made by or to the court and was endorsed with a penal notice informing the respondent that disobedience to the order would constitute a contempt of court and render them liable to be committed to prison (Order 29 r 1(3)). The advocate should have a copy of the order.

(b) The order has been served personally on the respondent (Order 29 r 1(2)(a)). The advocate should normally have an affidavit proving service (even in cases where the respondent was present when the order was made). The judge may dispense with the need for service (or proof of service) of the order where he or she (a) is satisfied that, pending service, the respondent has had notice of the order either by being present at the hearing or by being informed of its terms, or (b) thinks it just to do so (Order 29 rr 1(6) and 1(7)).

(c) An application to commit (or more accurately a notice to the respondent to show cause why a committal order should not be made against them) has been issued (Form N78). The application must state precisely and in detail the alleged breaches of the order. For example, a general allegation that the respondent has assaulted the applicant will not do. Details must be given of the nature of the assault, the time and place when it happened, who was there, what injuries were sustained and so on. The application should be supported by an affidavit setting out fully the grounds on which committal is sought in the same sort of detail.

NOTES:

(d) The application to commit has been served personally on the respondent at least two clear days before the hearing of the application. The supporting affidavit should be served with the application. The advocate should normally have an affidavit of service of the application. The judge does have power to dispense with service of the application but will only do so in exceptional circumstances and only when the the order has been breached. Again, this has to be specifically proved (Order 29 r 1(7)).

If the judge is satisfied of the above, he has the following options:

(a) Commit the respondent to prison (the maximum term is two years for breach of an injunction or undertaking). It is unlikely that the judge will make an order for committal to prison on the first application, particularly in family/matrimonial cases and will take the applicant's views into account; often they do not really want the respondent to be committed on the first occasion.

(b) A suspended committal order – the court can suspend on whatever terms it considers appropriate, the most common being that the committal is suspended as long as the respondent does not breach the order again. The sentence should be fixed as should any period of suspension. Activation of a suspended sentence is not automatic: the court has a discretion to change the sentence or discharge the suspended order altogether.

(c) A fine and/or an order that the respondent pay the costs of the hearing (possible even where the respondent is legally aided).

(d) Adjourn the application generally with liberty to restore. The applicant can then bring the matter back to court if

NOTES:

there is another breach by the respondent. If the respondent breaches the order a second time, they are far more likely to be committed.

(e) Change the terms of the original order. For example, the court could add a power of arrest to the order, or could widen the terms of the order.

(f) In Children Act cases, imprisonment is less likely to be ordered, particularly because the person in breach usually has day to day care of the child. The court may consider whether as a result of a persistent refusal to allow contact the child's residence should be changed.

Committal applications can be made *ex parte* where there is extreme urgency. This is very unusual and the judge will want good reasons why notice could not have been given to the respondent.

There are extensive and useful notes in the *Green Book*, under s 38 of the County Courts Act and under Order 29.

The application

Where? High Court/county courts/magistrates' courts

Who? High Court – High Court judge
County court – circuit judge
Magistrates' court – magistrates

Robes? Yes (save in magistrates' court)

Preliminaries

Committal applications are normally put at the top of the circuit judge's list. It is often difficult to predict in advance how long the hearing will take as it depends on whether the respondent turns up and what is in dispute.

You should ask your client whether there have been any recent developments. If there have been recent developments,

NOTES:

you should make your opponent aware of what you say they are if you intend to raise them although they cannot be relied on in support of the committal application. You should also check what it is that the applicant really wants. Especially in family cases and particularly where the parties have children, the applicant rarely wants the respondent to go to prison.

Your client may well need reassurance. The applicant may be worried about a violent reaction from the respondent, and the respondent may be worried about being put in prison.

In some cases, it will be possible to agree the facts with your opponent. This will speed up the application, and may save the applicant the trauma of having to give evidence in person (which may, tactically, be in the respondent's favour as well as the applicant's).

The applicant should always be present in person.

If the respondent appears but is not represented, the judge will, before the hearing starts, warn them of the possible outcome of the case and encourage them to get representation.

Hearing

This guide uses the example of a committal application following breach of a non-molestation order in the county court.

The applicant's advocate should introduce the parties, the application and the documents:

> *May it please your Honour, I appear for the applicant, Mrs Brain, my learned friend Mrs Twitchett appears for the respondent, Mr Brain. This is an application to commit the respondent to prison for breach of a*

non-molestation injunction, made against the respondent on 12 February of this year by His Honour Judge Black. Does your Honour have a copy of that order? Your Honour will see that the court ordered that: 'Mr Norman Brain is forbidden (whether by himself or by instructing or encouraging any other person) from assaulting, harrassing, pestering ....'. The standard penal notice is attached to the bottom of the order. Your Honour, there should be an affidavit of George Brown, a process server, in the court bundle proving service of the order on the respondent.

An application to commit was issued on 24 March and served on the respondent last Tuesday. Does your Honour have a copy of the application and the affidavit in support?

(Hand affidavit to judge.)

The supporting affidavit should set out the background facts and grounds for the application. It should not, therefore, be necessary to go over these at any length. The judge may, however, ask you to clarify one or two details. If there have been developments since the supporting affidavit was sworn, it may also be necessary to go through these.

If the respondent does not turn up, the judge may simply deal with the case on the applicant's affidavit though he or she is more likely to ask the applicant to give oral evidence.

If the respondent does appear and does not admit the breaches, the applicant will at least have to be tendered for cross-examination. The applicant's advocate may wish to expand on one or two matters in the affidavit, or deal with some recent developments, but detailed evidence-in-chief will not normally be necessary.

I call Mrs Brain.
Can you give the court your full name and address?

NOTES:

What is your occupation?

Mrs Brain, you swore an affidavit on 6 March. Can you look at this affidavit and tell the court if that is your signature on the last page?

Is there anything in it which you wish to retract or change?

I would just like you to clarify a couple of points. You say in paragraph 4 that Mr Brain hit you over the head with a flower pot. What happened between you just before he did that?

Has anything of significance happened between you and your husband since you swore your affidavit? What are you asking the court to do about your husband's behaviour?

Could you wait there, please, Mrs Brain; there may be some more questions.

The respondent's advocate will then cross-examine the applicant. Cross-examination should cover:

- any factual disputes between the parties;
- more detail as to the exact nature of the breaches or the circumstances leading up to the breaches;
- if the breaches are admitted, any extenuating circumstances (eg provocation) which could be used by the respondent in mitigation.

The respondent should always be given a chance to mitigate and explain why he or she has breached the order. In practice, particularly where breaches of the order are admitted, the judge often takes over the role of cross-examining the respondent and demanding an explanation for the breaches of the order.

Submissions should be fairly brief, unless there are many contested facts. The applicant's advocate should make clear what order the applicant is seeking.

NOTES:

The judge will almost certainly give judgment immediately. Advocates should record the findings of fact made by the judge, as these may be of use at a later date, particularly if the order is breached again. At the end of the proceedings, do not forget to ask for legal aid taxation and certificate for counsel, if appropriate.

What if ...?

The application is defective?

The judge has the power to waive most defects in the application, if minor. If the judge refuses to exercise his or her discretion, or it would be inappropriate to waive the defect, the advocate can ask for another hearing date allowing time to correct the defect. In some urgent cases, the judge may be persuaded to direct that the case be listed very quickly. You may need to ask for a continuation of the undertaking or injunction, if either is about to expire.

Breaches occur after the issue of the notice to show cause?

See the case of *Wright v Jess* [1987] 2 All ER 1067. The court may take the post-issue breaches into account. However, if time allows, a supplemental notice to show cause should be issued and served.

There are pending criminal proceedings?

There is no reason why the civil proceedings should wait until the criminal proceedings have been heard. Contempt proceedings should be dealt with swiftly and decisively. However, the court will usually consider an adjournment if the criminal proceedings will be heard in the near future, and the applicant's safety is protected in the meantime, for example, by bail conditions or because the respondent is in prison. If a sentence of imprisonment or other punishment has been imposed by the criminal courts, the respondent

NOTES:

will not necessarily be let off the hook by the civil court but it is likely to reduce the sentence imposed or the court might impose a concurrent sentence.

NOTES:

7 : Land law

The junior advocate tends to play a fairly humble role in land law cases: you are not likely to be tackling long and weighty trials in the Chancery Division. The Woolf Report recommends that all possession proceedings concerning residential property should start in a county court (with provision for transfer up in certain circumstances). This chapter is, therefore, mainly confined to county court procedure where most residential possession proceedings take place.

You might also encounter:

(a) Applications to suspend warrants for possession: see s 89 of the Housing Act 1980. Take note that if the tenant is in breach of a suspended possession order the tenancy may have come to an end (*Thompson v Elmbridge Borough Council* [1987] 1 WLR 1425). It may be that if, after the breach, the landlord has accepted further rent, the court will infer that the parties meant to create an entirely new tenancy (but see *Burrows v London Borough of Brent, The Times*, 4 November 1996 and *Greenwich LBC v Regan, The Times*, 9 February 1996).

    See also the general guidance in Chapter 4 on interlocutory applications.

(b) Applications to set aside a possession order: see the provisions of CCR Order 37.

(c) Disrepair actions: these follow the course of any normal trial. It frequently happens that a counterclaim for disrepair is produced at the last minute at a possession hearing. If the draft defence suggests disrepair on a scale proportionate with the arrears claimed, the court is

NOTES:

likely to adjourn the possession claim if it is based on rent arrears. If for the landlord, you may be able to resist if you can argue that, even taking into account the damages for disrepair, there would be substantial arrears such as to justify a possession order or argue that the money claim should be adjourned without affecting the possession claim, because arrears do not need to be proved to obtain possession, eg in a non-secure tenancy case. A useful book on the subject of disrepair is Luba, J, *Repairs: tenants' rights*, 3rd edn, Legal Action Group.

Possession actions

The landlord is nearly always seeking one or more of the following:

1. Order for possession (immediate or suspended);
2. Arrears of rent, and mesne profits (or damages for use and occupation, usually based on what the rent would have been, from judgment to actual possession);
3. Costs.

To be awarded arrears of rent, the landlord must show that there was an agreement for rent to be paid, and that rent has not been paid. The pleadings must give details of all payments due which have not been made, possibly in the form of a schedule (CCR Order 6 r 3).

The rules also require that the pleadings give details of the payment history (if the landlord's case is that payments are always late), the steps taken by the landlord to recover the rent, details of the tenant's personal and financial circumstances, if known, including benefit entitlement and any relevant details of the landlord's personal circumstances.

In practice, courts expect the 'social' landlords to know something about the tenant, and to have made efforts to

NOTES:

contact them, including attempting to visit them in the property.

To gain possession, the landlord must show that:

(a) he or she has superior title to the land (his right to possession);

(b) he or she is the tenant's landlord (under a lease or licence);

(c) the tenant's right to possession (the lease or licence) has been validly determined; and

(d) the landlord satisfies any special requirements (including in many cases within the Rent Acts, reasonableness) for an order for possession.

The tenant must try to show a flaw in one of these points (almost always under (c) and (d)), and draw attention to any technical deficiencies in the landlord's case, for example, by showing that the landlord did not comply with the time limit for service of notice, or that there is a serious defect in the notices (or they were not served at all), or that the arrears are disputed or arise out of housing benefit arrears, or that the landlord has refused to accept the rent, or that there is a counterclaim for disrepair.

Many residential tenants have some form of security of tenure under the Rent Act 1977, the Housing Act 1985 (public sector tenancies) or the Housing Act 1988 (referred to collectively as 'the Rent Acts'). These provisions are all set out fully in the *Green Book* under 'Residential Premises'. However, also note the important amendments made by the Housing Act 1996. The Protection from Eviction Act 1977 also applies to almost all residential tenancies and this too is set out in the same section of the *Green Book*.

NOTES:

If a residential tenancy falls within one of these codes, then the landlord cannot obtain an order for possession unless he can prove one of the grounds for possession prescribed by the relevant Act. Furthermore, in the case of many of the grounds, it is provided that possession will not be ordered unless it is reasonable.

In practice, possession will often not be granted for, say, arrears of rent, except on a suspended basis, ie the tenant can remain in occupation as long as they pay the contractual rent plus a certain sum off the arrears. If the landlord has made an agreement with the tenant for arrears to be paid off at a specific rate, then it will not be reasonable to make an order for possession while the tenant is keeping up with the agreed payments.

Where a suspended order is clearly appropriate, an application for an outright order will not be well received by the court. The advocate should be ready to justify any order which he or she seeks.

As to (c), residential leases and licences with security of tenure under the Housing Act 1985 or the Housing Act 1988 must (subject to dispensing provisions) be determined by notices of specific kinds prescribed by the Acts. Most other residential leases and licences must be determined by service of a valid notice to quit. There are very few exceptions such as where the landlord shares the residence with the defendant. The notice must comply with the provisions of the Protection from Eviction Act 1977: it must be in writing, contain the prescribed information and be given not less than four weeks before the date on which it is to take effect.

Where any of these notices are required, service must be proved – orally or by affidavit – by the person who served

NOTES:

the notice. In practice, the court often admits hearsay evidence of service (eg from a responsible officer for the local authority who has inspected the file) but strictly speaking they should not. See the *What if ...?* section below for further details.

The case must also be properly pleaded. If there is an error or omission in the particulars of claim, the plaintiff must ask for leave to amend (see CCR Order 15) and ask for re-service to be dispensed with. The defendant may argue that he or she is prejudiced by the amendment being made without notice or re-service and ask for an adjournment with costs to be paid by the plaintiff.

Business tenancies are regulated by the Part II of the Landlord and Tenant Act 1954 (in the *Green Book* under 'Business Premises'). Where a tenancy falls within Part II, the landlord may terminate it only by forfeiture (usually for breach of covenant) or by service of a notice under s 25 of the Act. The tenant may terminate by notice to quit or by surrender.

NB: Where a tenant has statutory protection under the Rent Act 1977, Housing Act 1985 or Housing Act 1988, the order cannot be made by agreement. One of the dangers from the tenant's point of view is that he or she may be considered to have made themselves voluntarily homeless if they consent to an order; another is that if a suspended possession order is breached, it may bring the tenancy to an end. If the two sides meet beforehand and agree on an appropriate order, the plaintiff must still prove their case in the usual way (though he or she can be assisted by admissions from the defendant, for example, that the notice to quit has been served). If a vital element is missing, there will be no order. A defendant may, of course, agree to leave the property, but such an agreement cannot be enforced.

NOTES:

Where the court has a discretion whether or not to grant possession, the judge will want to know as much as possible about the tenant. The landlord or housing officer should be ready to comment if possible on, for example, the tenant's entitlement to housing benefit (in rent arrears cases), whether the tenant is in work, whether he or she has children, and so on.

The Woolf Report has recommended a two-stage approach to possession proceedings which could be used by private landlords, but is really aimed at social landlords. It proposes that there be a paper hearing to deal with arrears of rent, at which the district judge would look at the information provided by the parties and consider whether to make an order that the tenant should repay the arrears and at what rate. At the second stage, if necessary, the landlord could apply for a possession order, which could, as now, be suspended on terms.

The Woolf Report also recommends that all possession hearings should be in chambers, with members of the public being admitted unless the parties objected.

Useful texts to take to court with you include: Colbey, R, *Residential Possession*, 3rd edn, 1996, Cavendish Publishing; Luba, Madge and McConnell, *Defending Possession Proceedings*, 3rd edn, 1993, Legal Action Group and Walter and Harris, *Claims to the Possession of Land*, 3rd edn, 1995, Tolley Publishing.

The application

Where? County court

Who? Circuit judge/district judge

Robes? Yes, except in mortgage possession actions or interlocutory hearings such as applications to suspend warrants or to set aside orders.

NOTES:

Preliminaries

The majority of residential possession applications are unopposed. These are listed in large numbers in what are often known as 'short' or 'undefended' possession lists. The courts hear dozens of applications in the course of a morning or afternoon. The expectation is that no case will take longer than five minutes, if that. If any hint of a triable issue emerges, the case will almost certainly be adjourned to a date when more time is available.

It follows that the presentation of such cases must be crisp and precise. If for the landlord, any purported but unfounded defence must be swiftly and convincingly shown to be groundless. If for the tenant, then the opposite holds true. If the case has to be adjourned, the court may make directions and you should be ready to suggest anything which you consider necessary. Where the application is opposed, it is heard in the same way as any civil trial.

Hearing

The example given below is of an application for possession of premises let on an assured tenancy under the Housing Act 1988 before the circuit judge. There is now a special paper procedure for some applications in respect of assured shorthold tenancies under that Act but sometimes an oral hearing will be required where the court is not satisfied with the level of detail in the application form or where there is a dispute about the service of a notice under s 20, a prerequisite to create this type of tenancy (although, from early 1977, note s 96 and schedule 7 of the Housing Act 1996, which abolish this rule for tenancies created subsequently).

NOTES:

The presentation of the case is as follows:

1. *Introduce the parties*
   May it please your Honour, I appear for the plaintiff in this matter and my learned friend Mr Motorway appears for the defendant.

2. *Open the case*
   This is a claim for possession of Flat 2, The Elms, Weybridge. The plaintiff's case is that the defendant has an assured tenancy under the Housing Act 1988 of the premises but that the plaintiff is now entitled to possession because of rent arrears under ground 8 of Schedule 2 of the Act. The plaintiff will also say that several agreements for payment of the arrears have fallen through.

3. *Call your witness*
   This will be the landlord, managing agent, housing officer – housing officers and managing agents should give their occupation as well as their name and business address.

4. *Prove title*
   Are you the (leasehold/freehold) owner/do you manage the premises at The Elms, etc?

In theory, you need to be able to prove this, for example, with the original of a lease, or office copies from the Land Registry. Court practice varies, but if the terms of the landlord's title are relevant to his right to possession (as, for example, with some non-secure tenancies), those terms must be proved. Otherwise, documents of title tend to be dispensed with.

Have you got a copy of the lease/office copy land registry entry giving you/showing your ownership of the premises?

Hand the lease/other document to the witness for identification, then hand it to the judge. If anything in

NOTES:

it is vital to the parties' rights to possession, draw this to the judge's attention.

Your Honour, may I just draw your attention to clause 3.

The judge will indicate when he or she has checked the document and you can continue.

5. *Prove the tenancy*
   Did you grant a tenancy of the premises to the defendant? When? Have you got a copy of the tenancy agreement?

Hand this up, and again the judge will indicate when you may go on. At this point, if any term of the tenancy agreement causes the tenancy to be non-secure, draw the judge's attention to it.

If rent arrears/mesne profits are claimed, ask the witness to state the amount of the current rent.

If the plaintiff's case is that a tenancy is in fact an assured shorthold, deal with the service of the s 20 notice at this point: was a notice served, when and how.

6. *Show a ground for possession*
   What is the current state of the rent account? Is the tenant up-to-date with the rent? What is the total amount owed by the tenant at today's date?

Be ready to hand up any documentary evidence.

Local authorities or housing associations often produce a rent book or a computer printout of the arrears. These print-outs can be difficult to understand. For example, the rent arrears are usually set out by week numbers instead of dates. If there is time, you should write out the details in a more understandable format or otherwise ask the relevant

NOTES:

witness to explain what the printout means. It really ought to be obvious from the particulars of claim so you may have to do some apologising.

7. *Show service of a notice to quit (or other statutory notice ending the right of occupation)*
   Did you serve a notice to quit on the tenant? Do you have a copy of the notice?

NB: You *must* prove service on each and every tenant against whom you seek a possession order. If the witness did not serve the notice, ask them who did. You will then need to have an affidavit of service from that person. Say:

> *Sir, there is an affidavit of service. Perhaps I can come to that in a moment.*

Finish examining the witness, then hand up the affidavit.

The judge's attention could now be drawn to any minor irregularity in the notice which he or she can be asked to waive. For more significant problems, see *What if ...?* below.

In opposed cases, the defendants or their representative may cross-examine the plaintiff's witness. If there is no opponent, simply continue:

> *Your Honour, I have no further questions for the witness. May he or she step down?*

Then, the tenant gives evidence and is cross-examined. After that give a closing speech.

If you are acting for the defendant, draw out – while cross-examining the plaintiff's witness, examining your witnesses and closing – any reasons why:

(a) the grounds for possession are not made out;

(b) the notice to quit or other essential notice is invalid or was not properly served; or

NOTES:

(c) where appropriate, why it would not be reasonable to make an order (eg housing benefit arrears, other payment due to be made to the tenant imminently, that the tenant has been paying something towards the arrears regularly and voluntarily and will continue to do so, any particular reasons why the arrears have built up, such as relationship breakdown) or why any order should be suspended: see s 89 of the Housing Act 1980.

If it is not possible to understand the schedule of rent arrears in the particulars of claim, you may be able to make something out of the confusion by showing that the landlord cannot prove exactly what is owed.

8. Close the case

Be ready with a page reference to the *Green Book* if the judge asks for it.

Summarise as briefly as possible:

> *I would ask for possession in ... days.*

(Section 89 of the Housing Act 1980 limits the court's discretion as to the time for possession in many cases.)

> *I am asking for an outright order in view of the high level of arrears, and the fact that several agreements to pay something towards the arrears have already broken down.*
>
> *Your Honour may, however, be minded to suspend the order. In that event, may I suggest ...*

For example, possession in 28 days suspended on payment of current rent plus £5 per week. If the tenant is unemployed, the 'usual' order at time of writing is for current rent plus £2.30 per week.

NOTES:

NB: If the relevant legislation requires reasonableness as a condition for possession, you should now say why it is reasonable for the court to make any order at all. The requirement applies to suspended orders as to outright ones. For example, where a tenant has persistently failed to stick to agreements, it could be suggested that the sanction of a court order is needed to provide an incentive to comply.

If the court has jurisdiction to suspend the order (s 89 Housing Act 1980) but you want an outright order, say why, for example, previous orders/arrangements have been disregarded.

Then say:

> *I also ask for judgment for the arrears, in the sum of £ ... , and mesne profits at the rate of £ ... per day.*

You must work out the current rent as a daily rate (this figure should be in the pleadings).

9. Costs

The judge will make an order, and then either ask you if you want anything else or simply pause and wait for you to deal with costs. Costs follow the event in the usual way. In quick possession actions, it is normal for the court to assess the costs as a fixed sum. If the defendant has not participated in the proceedings, nor put in a defence, see Appendix B to CCR Order 38 which sets out the prescribed rates. Otherwise, see CCR Order 38 rr 3D and19. Each court tends to have a 'going rate' for this, and you can ask for this sum. Pick this up from preceding cases in the list, or ask a colleague or member of court staff. The amount will not usually cover the costs which have been incurred but often it is simpler and quicker to accept a reduction and avoid taxation, especially when the reality is that the tenant is

NOTES:

unable to pay them in any event. When the time comes, stand up and say:

> *I ask for the plaintiff's costs, and I wonder if they might be assessed [at £175 or whatever].*

To ensure a timetable for payment of costs where a suspended possession order has been made, the plaintiff's advocate might add:

> *Could the costs be added to the arrears?*

If the defendant is legally aided, the order for costs is almost always not to be enforced without leave.

In practice, and particularly in respect of public sector tenancies, hearings are much shorter, especially if the judge or clerk has checked through the papers before the hearing. In one London county court, two questions are asked: 'What are the arrears?' and 'What do you know about the tenant?'

Special cases

Statutorily non-secure tenancies

In other words, tenancies falling within the express exceptions to the protection conferred by whichever Act would usually apply. In opening, the plaintiff should say:

> *The plaintiff contends that the tenant has no security of tenure by reason of [section, Act]. If I may, I shall deal with that matter in closing.*

Be ready, however, to explain if asked. Then, make sure that the evidence includes the matters necessary to prove that the exception applies.

Finally, in closing, say:

> *In my submission the tenant has no security of tenure by reason of (section, Act). May I assume that you are*

NOTES:

familiar with that provision or do you wish me to take your Honour through the provision in detail?

If the judge requires explanation, say:

That section appears in the Green Book *at page ...'*

or offer to hand up a photocopy.

Then, briefly state which facts you consider to bring the case within the exception.

Appearing for a tenant, conversely, call evidence as to facts which you say bring the case *outside* the exception, and then argue the point in closing. However, if the exception *does* apply, be sure that you know the extent of the court's powers to help your client, for example, by suspending or delaying a possession order. It will obviously not help to ask for relief which the court has no jurisdiction to give.

Squatters

There is a special accelerated procedure for obtaining possession against squatters and other trespassers (eg those who occupied the premises under a mere licence and refused to vacate on its termination) under Order 24 of the County Court Rules (RSC 113) (the Woolf Report recommends that the county court and High Court procedures be brought into line). The order also gives the court power to make an interim possession order against a trespasser (not a former tenant who has remained in occupation) when the only claim is for possession. In neither case can the landlord make a claim for mesne profits or damages for use and occupation. The application must be accompanied by an affidavit which states the plaintiff's interest in the land, the facts of the unlawful occupation, and the fact that the plaintiff does not know the name of any person occupying the land save those named in the application/summons. Each

NOTES:

named occupier must be personally served. Unnamed occupiers are served by leaving a copy of the papers at the premises. The defendants often do not attend. If they attend and bring any affidavit or make representations, the court decides whether any defence is disclosed. If so, it can be heard then and there if the issues are simple. If it is more complex, directions are given. The hearing is in open court in the county court; in the High Court it is usually in Chambers before a Master.

The case can be presented as follows:

> *May it please your Honour, I appear for the plaintiff. The defendants do not appear/are here in person. This is a claim under Order 24 for possession of premises at 1 Rabbit Road, Croydon. Has your Honour had a chance to look at the papers?*

The judge either will say yes, or will now look at the application and affidavit.

> *I am grateful. Your Honour will see that the plaintiff as freehold owner is entitled to possession, and that the defendants entered as trespassers and have refused to leave. They have been duly served with the papers. In the circumstances, I seek an order for possession forthwith.*

If the defendants have appeared, they will now be heard. A representative for the defendant should call any necessary evidence, explain to the judge why it amounts to a defence to the possession claim, and suggest directions. The most common argument is that the 'squatter' is in fact a 'tenant'. The owner's representative will attempt to show that there is no real defence. The judge will then make a decision. Following this, the advocate should deal with costs:

> *I am instructed to seek the plaintiff's costs. If Your Honour is minded to grant them, may I ask that they be assessed in the sum of £ ... .*

NOTES:

Say why costs should be awarded, eg the occupants were asked to leave on several occasions and warned that court action would follow, or they have damaged the property or harassed neighbouring occupiers, as the case may be.

Defendants' representatives, conversely, should bring to the attention of the court any hardship or other reason why costs should not be ordered.

What if ...?

The client wants to recover rent arrears but these have not been pleaded in the particulars of claim?

The rules have been specifically amended to require that details of rent arrears are spelt out where this is the ground for seeking possession so, in this sort of case, the court is going to be hostile to an application when this has not been done. You will probably have to ask for an adjournment to amend and re-serve. Where there are other grounds for seeking possession, the defect may not be so critical and, indeed, it may be that the arrears have arisen since the proceedings were issued. If you are for the landlord, you should explain the problem to your client and ask whether they actually want to pursue the rent arrears. This may be a tricky conversation as the landlord will want to know why the arrears have not been pleaded. Explain that if the landlord wants to pursue the arrears, there may have to be another hearing and extra costs will be involved (which are not likely to be recoverable from the tenant).

In court, the landlord's advocate should explain the position at the outset. Say that you wish, in any event, to ask the court to make an order for possession that day. Ask to amend your pleading so as to add the arrears claim. Ask the court whether it is prepared to deal with the arrears without

NOTES:

re-service. If the amended claim has to be re-served, ask the court to adjourn the claim for arrears.

The claim is wrongly pleaded in some other way, eg the address of the premises is slightly incorrect?

Again, deal with the problem in opening and ask the court to allow you to amend without re-service. If the tenant was served at the right address and was not misled, the problem is purely technical and the court is likely to be sympathetic. If not, the matter will be adjourned. Ask for costs to be reserved: again, this application may or may not succeed.

The person who served the notice to quit is not in court to give evidence?

An affidavit of service is usually acceptable (CCR Order 20 rr 6 and 7). But, if you lack even this, problems may arise. Hearsay evidence is admissible under s 2 of the Civil Evidence Act 1968, subject to notice procedures. Where no defence has been served, the notice procedures do not apply unless the court directs that they should: CCR Order 20 r 15(2). In other cases, the court has a discretion to disapply the notice procedures and admit the evidence: Order 20 r 20. Some judges will in their discretion accept hearsay evidence of service, for example, from a housing officer who knows that a colleague served the notice. Many will not, on the principle that a person should not be made potentially homeless except on the best evidence.

If you have no evidence or unsatisfactory hearsay evidence, the court will adjourn. Mention the problem in opening and leave your options open, for example:

> *The only evidence of service is in the form of hearsay. If, in your discretion you were willing to accept it, the matter could proceed. Otherwise, I shall of course have to request an adjournment.*

NOTES:

There is one other solution. If the defendant is in court, he or she may admit receiving the notice. It is worth asking, though with an unrepresented defendant your difficulty should be explained frankly; it can be pointed out that if the case is adjourned, the defendant will have to come back to court on another occasion.

There is no evidence of the landlord's title?

In most short cases none is required, save where the nature of the landlord's title specifically affects the tenant's rights (eg in a non-secure tenancy under Schedule 1 to the Housing Act 1985). It is worth asking whether the judge will accept oral evidence. Once again, the problem may be solved if the defendant attends the hearing. He or she may admit that the landlord is the landlord. You could invoke the established rule that a tenant is estopped from disputing his landlord's title but this is a fairly obscure argument which is not well-liked by the courts. A general denial of the landlord's allegation does not amount to a denial of title. If these solutions fail, you will have to request an adjournment.

In a case of a pre-1977 shorthold tenancy, the section 20 notice is missing?

It is unlikely that a defendant who turns up to court will then admit having been given the notice. However, it is worth a try. Otherwise, this is a fatal flaw. The only solution would be to show that the landlord is in any event entitled to possession even if it is an assured tenancy, provided you can get over any deficiencies in the pleadings.

The tenant pleads an arguable defence to the possession claim, but rent arrears are mounting fast?

An adjournment can be made on conditions. It is not unusual to adjourn a case on the condition that a certain amount is paid by way of rent in the meantime.

NOTES:

Mortgage possession actions

Reference should be made to Order 6 rr 5 and 5A for the procedural requirements, s 21 County Courts Act 1984, s 36 Administration of Justice Act 1970 and s 8 Administration of Justice Act 1973 (set out in the notes to s 21 County Courts Act 1984).

CCR Order 6 r 5 specifies the information which the particulars of claim must contain and further details are required by Order 6 r 5A, if the property is a dwelling house. Your first task is, therefore, to check that the required details have been provided. This information must be verified on affidavit.

You should also have available at court the charge certificate and a recent land registry or charges register search. Often copies are exhibited to the affidavit. You will need to scrutinise the figures carefully so that you understand how the 'arrears' figures is calculated. If you are representing the mortgagor, this may be a good line of attack. If the plaintiff cannot prove the arrears as alleged this might at least win some extra time for the defendant.

Otherwise, it is most often a question of satisfying the court that the defendant will be able to repay the overdue sums within a reasonable time. In theory, this could mean the remainder of the mortgage term. Practice varies between courts; some district judges look for repayment within a year, others will allow up to three years. The more specific your evidence that the money will be repaid, the more likely the court, and possibly the plaintiff, will favour a longer period of suspension. For example, if the defendant is hoping to get a new job, details of the steps he or she has taken should be given, or if the defendant has already found a new job, copies of wage slips or an employment contract

NOTES:

are a great help. It often happens that the mortgagor's evidence is not yet ready and you have to ask for an adjournment. Again, the more specific you can be about what will be achieved/found out during any period of an adjournment, the more likely it is to be granted. Even if you do not have the evidence in affidavit form, the court will usually take some notice of it.

One problem frequently encountered is DSS arrears, as it is often difficult to get information from the DSS. You may need to give full details of the efforts which have been made on behalf of or by the defendant to communicate with the DSS.

Obviously, if you have sufficient advance warning of the hearing you should find out whether the mortgagee will look favourably on a request for an adjournment or suspended possession order on terms. Two problems often arise. The first is that the mortgagee often cannot be contacted directly because the matter is in the hands of their solicitors, and having to go through the solicitors means the whole process takes longer. The second is that the mortgagee's solicitors often appear by agents who have no instructions or parameters within which to negotiate. In this case, you will have to do your best to persuade the court to give the defendant some leeway.

One other argument that can be advanced for postponing the possession order is to allow the defendant time to put the property on the market themselves (see *Palk v Mortgage Services Funding plc* [1993] Ch 331; *Target Home Loans Ltd v Clothier* [1994] 1 All ER 439 and *Barrett v Halifax Building Society* [1995] NPC 146).

It should be noted that the existence of a counterclaim or set off against the mortgagee is not a defence and will not of

NOTES:

itself be enough to persuade the court to exercise its powers to adjourn or suspend. Evidence is required to show that the defendant is likely to be able to repay the debt, ie that proceedings have been started, that the prospects of success are good, that the defendant would put the money towards the mortgage arrears: you will have to consult the numerous cases on this point, including *Ashley Guarantee plc v Zacaria* [1993] 1 All ER 254.

One currently popular defence is to allege that the defendants or one of them was unduly influenced to enter into the mortgage. This has given rise to a spate of litigation since the landmark decision of *Barclays Bank v O'Brien* [1993] 4 All ER 417. If you think you may be able to run this line of defence, you will undoubtedly need an adjournment to a much longer hearing time. Be prepared to ask for any necessary directions.

An extremely useful book to take to court is Brimelow, P and Clayton, N, *Mortgage Possession Actions*, 1st edn, 1994, Longmans.

Preliminaries

Many mortgage possession proceedings are unopposed; it is common for the defendant to turn up but often he or she does not have an argument to put to the court.

Mortgage possession actions tend to be dealt with in chambers by a district judge. It is rare for there to be oral evidence. Court practice varies considerably; some district judges hear the cases in their own chambers one by one, though in fairly rapid succession. Some district judges, particularly in the busier courts, hear the cases in a court room, but sitting down at the front, with those waiting to be heard sitting at the back and coming forward when the case is called.

NOTES:

On first listing, it is usually assumed that the case will not take very long. If it transpires that more time is needed the case will be adjourned.

Hearing

If you are for the mortgagee, introduce yourself and the defendant, if present. Ensure that the court has your affidavit or hand it up. Allow the district judge time to read it through and answer any questions to the best of your ability. Often the court will want to know about any communication between the parties about the arrears and whether any offers have been made, or indeed, any repayments, and what the mortgagee knows about the defendant's personal circumstances.

Ask for the order you want (including a money judgment). In most cases, the mortgage will provide that costs are to be added to the security, in which case, tell the district judge this so it can be noted on the order. Otherwise, ask for your costs.

If the defendant attends, you can either tell the court what the defendant's position is (assuming you know this) and make any relevant submissions. Sometimes, however, and, of course, when you do not know the defendant's position, it is easier to let the defendant or their representative make their points and then reply to them.

If you represent the defendant, you simply explain to the court the nature of your defence, in the unlikely event that there is one, or why the court should exercise its discretionary powers under the Administration of Justice Act, with reference to any affidavit or other evidence you might have. Explain clearly how the defendant can make repayments, how much and over what timescale. Outline

NOTES:

the order you are asking the court to make and any consequential directions.

In theory, a certificate for counsel is not required because the hearing is not an interlocutory one, but if you are in doubt, for example, because the case has been adjourned and not finally decided, it never does any harm to ask for one.

NOTES:

8 : Employment

In this chapter we are particularly concerned with applications to industrial tribunals. Junior advocates are frequently instructed for such hearings. No doubt this is partly because costs are not recoverable for many such applications, and legal aid is generally not available. Litigants are, therefore, more than usually concerned to keep costs to a minimum.

The claims most frequently seen in industrial tribunals are for unfair dismissal or redundancy, under the Employment Rights Act 1996 (ERA) and for Sexual or Racial Discrimination, under the Equal Pay Act 1970, the Sex Discrimination Act 1975 or the Race Relations Act 1976.

Claims for unfair dismissal or for a redundancy payment can generally only be brought by those who have been continuously employed for more than 16 hours per week for at least two years. There is no minimum period of employment for a claim under the Equal Pay Act. For claims under the Sex Discrimination Act or the Race Relations Act, the complainant need have no contract of employment at all. Nor is there any minimum period of employment for claims for wrongful dismissal (as to which see below).

Industrial tribunals also have concurrent jurisdiction with the ordinary courts to hear claims for damages for breach of an employment or related contract and for claims for sums due under an employment contract up to a limit of £25,000 which may be brought by the employee or employer (by way of counterclaim only). This jurisdiction is governed by the Industrial Tribunals Extension of Jurisdiction Order 1994. There are a number of excluded claims such as damages in respect of personal injuries and others which are

NOTES:

listed in Article 5 of the Order, such as claims relating to restraint of trade clauses. The Order applies to employment which terminated after 12 July 1994.

Under the Order, the industrial tribunals can now hear claims for wrongful dismissal as well as unfair dismissal. Wrongful dismissal means dismissal in breach of contract, ie without the requisite notice period or pay in lieu and is no different from any other claim for breach of contract. The claimant must prove that there was a contract, that the contract contained a relevant term, and that the employer acted in breach of the term. An employee is then entitled to be put into the position he would have been in had the contract been properly performed. Normally, this will mean damages to compensate for the amount of pay in lieu to which the employee was entitled if the contract had been lawfully terminated. If the notice period would have carried the employee over the two-year qualifying period for rights under ERA (eg to claim for unfair dismissal), the damages may include a sum to compensate for the loss of these rights. Whether or not the contract expressly provides for a notice period, minimum notice periods are imported by ERA, s 86(1). The contract may provide for a more generous notice period and, in special circumstances, there may be an implied term providing longer notice.

It is a defence to a wrongful dismissal claim to show that the employee was dismissed for 'gross misconduct'.

If claims are brought for both wrongful and unfair dismissal, note that there can be no double recovery. Damages for breach of contract should be deducted from the relevant head of compensation for unfair dismissal, or vice versa.

Claims arising out of redundancy are also heard by the industrial tribunal. The rules for redundancy not involving

NOTES:

unfair dismissal are set out in Part XI of ERA. Essentially, where a qualifying employee is dismissed for redundancy as defined by ERA, s 135, he or she is entitled to a redundancy payment. The amount of this is the same as for a 'basic award' for unfair dismissal (see below). The claim must be brought within six months of the 'effective date of termination' (see below). Furthermore, if the employee was selected for redundancy unfairly or in a procedurally unfair way (including a failure to consult), not genuinely made redundant or the employer did not make reasonable efforts to find suitable alternative employment, the claim may be accompanied by a claim for unfair dismissal.

In this chapter, we deal principally with unfair dismissal. The procedure can be adapted for the other kinds of claim which the industrial tribunal has jurisdiction to hear.

Employment law is closely controlled by statute. In particular, be aware of time limits and other procedural rules. Many claims are decided on the basis of these.

Unfair dismissal

The applicant seeking a remedy for his unfair dismissal will submit an originating application (Form IT1) to the Central Office of Industrial Tribunals (COIT). The respondent must, within 14 days, enter a notice of appearance stating whether or not he intends to oppose the application on Form IT3, specifying the grounds upon which the application is opposed. In a case of unfair dismissal, the respondent must state whether or not it is conceded that there was a dismissal and, if there was, the relevant statutory reason for the dismissal.

The time limit for making an application to the COIT is three months from the 'effective date of termination' (six months for unfair dismissal redundancy payments and, in cases of discrimination, three months from the last act complained of). The tribunal's discretion to hear late applications in unfair dismissal cases will be exercised only where it was not 'reasonably practicable', in all the circumstances, for the complaint to be made within the time limit. Ignorance of the provisions contained in employment protection legislation does not, in general, constitute a valid reason for extending the time limit, even if caused by bad legal advice.

The 'effective date of termination' is defined by s 97(1) ERA: generally, if dismissal is with notice, it is the date on which the notice expires. If there is no notice, it is the date on which the termination takes effect. In cases of fixed term contracts, it is the date on which the term expires.

An application may be made for further particulars of the other party's case and must be made in writing to the other party or, with a copy to the tribunal or, where the other party does not co-operate, to the tribunal. An application for further particulars should be distinguished from discovery. The latter discloses supporting evidence whilst the former clarifies the case. If the respondent refuses to produce a relevant document in their possession, the applicant may apply to the tribunal for an order for discovery. Such relevant documents include, for example, the letter of appointment; the contract of employment; the employer's disciplinary rules and procedures; any written warnings or minutes of disciplinary hearings and the letter of dismissal.

The bundle of the documents for the hearing will normally be compiled by the respondent. If the bundle is not agreed by the applicant, he may prepare his own bundle for use at the hearing. Bundles must be clearly presented. They should be properly paginated and indexed. At least five copies

NOTES:

must be made available (three for the tribunal, one for the other party and one for witnesses). Likewise, any party intending to raise a matter of law should provide a sufficient number of copies of any authority relied upon. Moreover, where possible, a list of authorities should be served both on the tribunal and on the other side a reasonable time before the hearing.

The Advisory, Conciliation and Arbitration Service (ACAS) is under a statutory duty to attempt to promote a settlement of a complaint. Copies of Form IT1 and IT3 are, therefore, sent to ACAS. If a settlement is reached, neither party can subsequently re-instate or continue proceedings. If the case is not settled, any material disclosed to ACAS will be deemed privileged and will not be disclosed to the tribunal.

The tribunal has jurisdiction to order reinstatement or re-engagement, but this is often impracticable because of acrimony. The usual remedy is compensation. This consists of a 'basic award' calculated according to rules in s 118 ERA and based on length of service, and a compensatory award (s 123 ff) for his or her provable financial loss as a result of dismissal. The calculation of this should take into account lost wages up to the time of finding a new job or up to the hearing and, if the claimant is still unemployed at the date of hearing, an estimate of how long he is likely to remain unemployed. Any contractual fringe benefits, for example, car, bonus, loans, pension, etc should be valued and included. The claimant must show that he or she has done their best to find a new job by way of producing job applications, etc. There is also an award for loss of statutory protection, ie the two years in a new job until the applicant will have full rights under the ERA. This is now usually put at £150–£250. It is also possible to claim for the expense of looking for work.

NOTES:

A number of deductions may have to be made. If the employee receives a redundancy payment which exceeds the amount of the basic award, the excess should be deducted from the compensatory award. So should any payment in lieu of notice. The tribunal has jurisdiction to reduce the compensatory award by such percentage as it considers just and equitable if it finds that the employee's conduct contributed to the dismissal: ERA, s 123(6).

After any deductions, the compensatory award is subject to a ceiling, currently £11,300. This is revised from time to time and should be checked. There is no ceiling in sex discrimination cases.

Special or additional awards (under s 125 ERA) are available in cases of dismissal for trade union membership or failure to comply with an order of re-engagement or reinstatement.

Industrial tribunal cases, like any other civil cases, can be settled 'out of court'. Settling is a particularly good idea in these cases, not only because of the usual saving in costs but also because of the rules on recoupment of state benefits. In most cases of unfair dismissal, the applicant will have claimed unemployment benefit or income support (jobseeker's allowance) during his time without a job. Meanwhile, if the claim succeeds, the tribunal will award compensation for the loss of wages for this period. The tribunal is required to identify the portion of the award which represents lost wages. The authorities then 'recoup' that amount from the employer, and the employee receives only the balance of the award. However, if the parties settle out of court and the settlement does not breakdown the settlement as between the basic and compensatory awards, it is possible to avoid the recoupment provisions.

So, the recoupment regulations in these cases effectively create room for negotiation. A compensation figure can be

NOTES:

agreed which, for the employee, will be more than he would have received after recoupment, and which, for the employer, will be less than the amount he would have had to pay including the recoupment figure. However, remember that you must have the client's permission before you attempt to negotiate a settlement. The client must understand that if there is a settlement, he or she will not have the satisfaction of a written decision from the tribunal.

Even if the matter goes to a full hearing, once the tribunal has found for the applicant, it can still be worthwhile for both parties to ask the tribunal to adjourn the case so that quantum can be agreed and more often than not the hearing on remedies is adjourned. An out-of-court agreement on a figure may avoid the recoupment provisions. Some tribunals very helpfully make known the basis on which they would be minded to calculate compensation (useful where there is future loss which is difficult to quantify) and then offer the parties time in which to negotiate.

A number of shorter hearings may precede the full hearing. These are:

1. *Pre-Hearing Assessment:* The purpose of a Pre-Hearing Assessment (PHA) is for the tribunal to assess either party's prospects of success. Consideration is given by the tribunal to Forms IT1 and IT3 and to any submissions made. Both parties are entitled to attend such hearings. Frequently, only the party with the weaker case normally attends. If the tribunal concludes that the party against which the application is made has no reasonable prospects of success, it cannot dismiss the case but will warn that party that it may be held liable for the other side's costs and may insist on that party paying a deposit of up to £150. The tribunal which hears the full case (which must be differently constituted from

NOTES:

the one which heard the PHA) is not, however, bound to order costs against that party, and it must consider the reasons which were given at the PHA for concluding that the party had no reasonable prospects of success before making a costs order.

2. *Preliminary Point or Preliminary Hearing:* The purpose of hearing a preliminary point is for the tribunal to consider whether it has jurisdiction to hear the full complaint. If, for example, the respondent alleges that the applicant had no reason to make his application out of time, the question will be determined as a preliminary point. The procedure follows that of a full hearing and both sides, including witnesses, normally attend. The burden of proof is on the respondent to show that the application was out of time. Then, the applicant has to show that it was not reasonably practicable to comply with the time limit.
3. *Directions Hearing:* Directions hearings are similar to those in a county court. These will be held to determine, for example, whether an order for further particulars or for discovery should be made. Such hearings are normally before the Chairman sitting alone who is not thereby disqualified from presiding over the substantive hearing. The party seeking a particular direction should simply introduce themselves and their opponent, state what directions he or she seeks, and explain why. The Chairman will then hear the other side, and the applicant may then reply, before the Chairman announces what directions he or she has decided to make.
4. *Interim Relief Hearing:* These are rare, and are not dealt with in this book.

A very useful and practical book on this subject is Kibling and Lewis, *Employment Law: An Adviser's Handbook*, 3rd edn,

NOTES:

1996, Legal Action Group. For a detailed analysis of the case law and statutes, read *Harvey on Industrial Relations*, Butterworths.

The application

Where?	Industrial Tribunal
Who?	A tribunal (normally a legally qualified Chairman and two lay 'wing members')
Robes?	No

Preliminaries

On arrival, go to the Applicants' or Respondents' waiting room as appropriate. A clerk will come to ask you whether you have any documents or legal materials for the tribunal.

If either party fails to attend, the tribunal may adjourn the case, hear it in the absence of the party or dismiss it. The party present may apply for costs.

Hearings are generally held in public and all the parties (including the advocates) remain seated throughout. The clerk will usually tell you where the parties should sit.

In theory, the tribunal can decide its own procedure but in practice hearings are often rather more formal than informal. However, rules of evidence do not apply in the same rigid manner. All relevant evidence is admissible, including hearsay evidence but this, of course, may carry considerably less weight. Witness statements may be read without formal notice if the parties agree.

Hearing

Once the clerk has identified the parties present, the Chairman may make some brief introductory remarks explaining how he or she likes things done and the procedure to be adopted, which should give you a clue as to the formality expected.

NOTES:

The Chairman (and each Wing Member) should be addressed as Sir/Madam. Remarks to the tribunal are conventionally addressed to the Chairman. The tribunal as a whole is referred to as 'you' in the second person and 'the tribunal' in the third person (or 'you and your colleagues').

Although the Chairman may ask either side to open the case, the party bearing the burden of proof will normally do so. It will, therefore, be the respondent who opens in the most frequently encountered cases, namely those in which dismissal is admitted but the unfairness of the dismissal is denied. In almost all other cases, the applicant will open the case. Any preliminary applications (eg to amend Form IT1 or IT3) should also be made at this point.

The advocate opening the case will then begin: (for the purposes of this work, it will be assumed that Mrs Puddleduck is claiming she was unfairly dismissed by her employers. It will, therefore, be for the employer (the respondent) to prove the fairness of the dismissal).

> *This is a claim by Mrs Puddleduck for compensation on the grounds of unfair dismissal. The date of dismissal was on 14 February 1994 and is not in dispute. As you will see from Form IT3, the reason for dismissal was Mrs Puddleduck's conduct.*

The advocate should briefly set out the contents of both forms fully to explain the issues of the case. It is always a good idea to familiarise the tribunal with the bundle at an early stage. Refer, therefore, to any important documents and outline the evidence you propose to call. If there are any esoteric words or phrases, it is best to explain them to the tribunal at the outset. Whilst it is crucial to paint a full and sufficiently detailed picture of the case, be guided by the reactions of the tribunal. It may be that it already regards

NOTES:

itself adequately aware of the points involved. The Chairman will usually let you know if he or she wants help on a particular point. Remember always what you are trying to establish. In cases of unfair dismissal, for example, the employer must prove that there was a reason for the dismissal, that this reason related to the capability or conduct of the applicant, illegality, redundancy or any other substantial justification and that he acted reasonably in the circumstances.

Having opened the case, call the evidence:

> *Would you give the tribunal your full name and address?*
> *What is your occupation?*
> *Did you once employ Mrs Puddleduck?*

Go through the history of the applicant's employment, highlighting any pertinent aspects, for example, past reprimands; staff re-organisation; codes of practice; rules of procedure, etc. Introduce the evidence to support the allegations in form IT3 and to rebut those in form IT1. Prove the reason for dismissal and the facts which made it a reasonable reason. Where you are appearing for an employer, you must draw out any facts which show that the employer was well aware of the rules and that he or she abided by them in dealing with the employee. Also, you must highlight any problems which the employee caused, or other reasons which made it fair to dismiss the employee.

The usual sequence of examination-in-chief followed by cross-examination and re-examination is followed.

When cross-examining the employer, obviously enough, you must try to show ways in which the employer fell short of the requirements of statute. Take the employer through any disciplinary rules used by them or the company and

NOTES:

probe any unfamiliarity with them. If you know that the employer broke a particular rule, ask them to read it out and then ask them to say how they complied with it. Explore any alternative solution which the employer could have tried but neglected. Try to get the employer to admit that he or she did not do everything possible to avoid dismissal. Where the facts of the employee's behaviour are in dispute, cross-examination must of course address credibility. Highlight any doubts or vagueness in the employer's version of events.

It is usual to conclude your case with words such as:

> *That is the case for the respondent.*

The other side may make a submission of no case to answer, if appropriate. This is only very rarely done and normally only if the tribunal has given an informal indication relating to the evidence called.

Only in exceptional cases does the applicant make an opening speech. Most of the time, the applicant's advocate will simply call the evidence. The sequence is the same as that for the respondent. As to content, the opposite arguments apply as for the employer. Prove, if necessary, that there was a dismissal. Attempt to show that the reason claimed by the employer was not the real reason, or that in the circumstances dismissal for that reason was not reasonable. Remember that a dismissal can be unfair for purely procedural reasons.

Having presented all the evidence, the advocate closes the applicant's case in the usual way:

> *That concludes the case for the applicant.*

Most often, the first closing speech is made by the applicant. Closing speeches should be succinct. Remind the tribunal

---

NOTES:

only of the main points of the case. Identify the strengths and weaknesses of the evidence and explain the principal issues. Finally, refer to any relevant law and spell out how the burden of proof has or has not been discharged. Refer the tribunal to any authorities but make sure you have enough copies available. Do not overburden the tribunal with law. If the only real issue between the parties concerns the facts of what happened, then stick to the facts. The tribunal will already be familiar with mainstream employment law, eg the definition of dismissal, the statutorily fair reasons, etc and you will not need authorities for these.

At the end of the hearing, the tribunal will usually either ask the parties to retire or will itself retire to deliberate. It may give its decision immediately or may reserve judgment. A short summary of the reasons for its decision will be given. Where a party intends to appeal to the Employment Appeal Tribunal (EAT), it is necessary to obtain full reasons for the tribunal's decision. Any appeal must be lodged within 42 days of receipt of the full reasons. An appeal will only lie on a point of law (though this can include in a suitably clear case that the findings of fact were not supported by the evidence). If no point of law is disclosed, it will be rejected. A party then has 28 days to appeal against rejection.

Other than for exceptional reasons, the tribunal will not award costs to either party. If the tribunal is of the opinion that a party has acted frivolously, vexatiously or otherwise unreasonably or has, for example, caused unnecessary adjournments, it may award costs.

The tribunal also has the power to grant allowances to the parties and witnesses to cover any expenses incurred by attendance at the hearing, except that a party against whom a costs order is made may not claim an allowance, these allowances are granted regardless of success or failure.

NOTES:

What if ...?

What if Form IT1 or IT3 contains a mistake or an omission?

An application to amend may be made at the outset once the clerk has identified the parties. Small amendments will usually be allowed.

If the tribunal gives an early indication as to its decision, is it still possible to settle the case?

Yes. As discussed above, cases may be amenable to settlement even after the tribunal has, in effect, made its decision. Although this is something of a 'staged' scenario, such an outcome will be to the financial benefit of both parties by avoiding the recoupment provisions. Advocates should not hesitate, therefore, to ask for an adjournment, even at the eleventh hour.

What if the client fails to provide adequate evidence of financial loss?

This can of course happen in any sort of case, but happens very regularly in industrial tribunals. Applicants are often (understandably) obsessed with the rights and wrongs of their dismissal or other grievance. It can be hard for them to focus on the practicalities of producing payslips, evidence of job applications, etc for the calculation of compensation. They may not have kept the necessary paperwork. We suggest two solutions. Firstly, if you discover well before the hearing that the evidence will not be available, use an application for discovery to obtain as much information about matters such as the applicant's salary from the other side. Secondly, if on the day you simply do not have enough to go on, ask for an adjournment after the decision on liability has been announced. Then explain the problem to your opponent, remind them of the advantages of settlement, and point out that, if no agreement is reached, the parties will

NOTES:

have to return another day. The employer, having lost the case, and faced with the possibility of having to return to the tribunal, will be well advised to settle. However, remember that, if you cannot prove your loss, the amount you recover will be that much less. Also, your client could be at risk as to the costs of an avoidable adjournment to another day. The amount you seek must be adjusted accordingly.

Notes:

9 : Insolvency

The most common insolvency applications which a junior advocate will encounter are petitions to wind-up companies and personal bankruptcy petitions and applications to set aside statutory demands. We deal with these three areas in this chapter.

These petitions and applications are governed mainly by the Insolvency Act 1986 and the Insolvency Rules 1986 ('IR') and the applications are quite different from any other type of hearing. The notes at the beginning of each section are not intended to be a detailed exposition of the law, merely a handy summary covering the areas most frequently encountered in practice. As a general rule, be careful. Insolvency is a highly specialised area and, however simple your case seems, you must make every effort to get a grasp of the overall picture.

Winding-up petitions

Where a creditor is owed money by a company and that company is unable to pay its debt, the creditor may apply to the court to have that company 'wound up'. Reference should be made to s 117 of the Act and Part 4 of the Rules. Section 122(1) of the Act sets out the grounds on which a company can be wound up by the court. The most relevant for our purposes is that provided under sub-section (f), namely that the company is unable to pay its debts. A creditor who is owed more than the minimum financial limit, currently £750, is entitled to file a petition to wind-up a company which owes him money; such a company is described as a 'debtor company'. They may be a 'trade creditor' or a 'judgment creditor'. The latter is a creditor who has

NOTES:

obtained judgment against the debtor company but the sums due under that judgment have not been paid and it has not been possible to enforce the judgment. A trade creditor is, essentially, anybody who is owed money by the debtor company. Although companies may be wound up in respect of unliquidated debts (see *Re Tweeds Garages Limited* [1962] Ch 406), if the fact of the debt is in dispute, this must be determined before a company can be wound up. The procedure, as stated above, is governed by the Insolvency Rules. Various documents must/may be filed before the application can be made.

(a) Statutory demand: this is a formal demand requesting the monies due. It is not essential to serve a statutory demand and if one is not served it will not prevent the application going ahead. However, a statutory demand is usually served when the petition is brought by a trade creditor. A company will be deemed unable to pay its debts if the demand is not met within three weeks of service. An error in the statutory demand will not always be fatal.

(b) Petition: this document is the formal application to wind up the debtor company. Three copies of the petition must be filed in the registrar's office.

(c) Affidavit verifying petition: this is an affidavit made by the petitioner or an employee or officer of the petitioner verifying the matters detailed in the petition.

(d) Affidavit of service of the petition: this affidavit must be sworn by the person who effected service stating the method of service. Ideally, this should be by personal service at the registered office of the company or on a director, other officer or employee (see IR 4(8)).

NOTES:

(e) Advertisement: the petition must be advertised in the Gazette at least seven days before the hearing and not less than seven days after service of the petition.

(f) Certificate of compliance: the petitioner or their solicitor must file in court a certificate of compliance at least five days before the hearing. This certificate should state the dates of the presentation and service of the petition, the date of the advertisement and the hearing date. The deponent should certify that the petitioner has complied with the Insolvency Rules.

(g) List of creditors: the petitioner should produce a list of the creditors who support or oppose ('opposing/supporting creditors') the petition at the hearing. If there are no other interested creditors, there will be no need to produce a list.

(h) Affidavit in opposition: usually there will not be any such affidavit but, if an opposing creditor or debtor wishes to file an affidavit, this must be done not less than seven days before the hearing date and a copy should be sent to the petitioner forthwith.

An invaluable book to have at court with you is Sealy and Milman, *Annotated Guide to the Insolvency Legislation*, 4th edn, 1994, CCH Editions Limited.

Hearing

Where? High Court (RCJ and district registries in Birmingham, Bristol, Cardiff, Leeds, Liverpool, Manchester, Newcastle upon Tyne and Preston) (all companies). County courts with jurisdiction in bankruptcy (not very many of them, see the list at the back of the *Green Book*) (companies with a share capital below £120,000) and in whose jurisdiction the company has a registered office

NOTES:

Who?	High Court – Registrar of the companies court (Sir/Madam) district registries and county courts – district judge (Sir/Madam)
Robes?	Yes

Preliminaries

In London, winding-up applications ('winders') are usually heard in open court en masse on a Wednesday in half-hour blocks commencing at 10.30 am. The advocate should obtain a copy of the daily cause list before the hearing so that he knows when their case is about to be called. This is important because in the companies court the ushers do not take the names of the advocates prior to the hearing; nor do they call all the cases in at 10.30 am. The associate calls the number and name of the case in court, in the order published in the daily cause list. The case will be called twice in quick succession, and if there is no response the petition will be dismissed.

Before the start of the half-hour block in which the advocate's case appears, he should call the name of the case in the court corridor to see if there are any other interested parties. The petitioning creditor's advocate should note the names of any interested parties as it will be their job to introduce them.

The court room itself can appear very intimidating on a first appearance; it will be full of advocates, many of whom will be very senior and very experienced in this kind of work. If you are unable to find a seat, attempt to stand as near to the front as possible to ensure that you are heard.

Hearing

The ordinary application is for the 'usual compulsory order'. This is an order that the company be wound up and that the company must pay the petitioner's costs.

NOTES:

(A) Judgment creditor's petition

This is a judgment creditor's petition in the sum of £7,777 odd. The debtor company is not represented and the list is clear.

So far as I am aware, sir, the documents are in order. I therefore ask for the usual compulsory order.

Note: The figure never includes the pence owed, this is referred to as 'odd'.

(B) Trade creditor's petition

This is a trade creditor's petition in the sum of £7,777 odd pursuant to a statutory demand.

(Continue as in (a) above.)

(C) Debtor company represented and two supporting creditors

This is a judgment creditor's petition in the sum of £7,777 odd.

The debtor company is represented by my learned friend Mr Jarvis. There are two supporting creditors. ABC Limited in the sum of £1,000 represented by my learned friend Mr Barrowclough and XYZ PLC in the sum of £2,222 odd represented by my learned friend Miss Singh.

(Continue as in (a) above. The debtor's representative will make submissions and then you will be given an opportunity to respond. The supporting creditors' representatives may also make submissions.)

(D) Defects in documents

The registrar may be prepared to waive small defects such as the advertisement being a day late or a small error in the spelling of the name of the debtor on one of the affidavits. The defect should be drawn to the registrar's attention and he or she should be asked to waive it.

NOTES:

(Begin as in (a) above.)

The documents are in order save that the advertisement was published one day late. Sir, would you waive that defect and grant the usual compulsory order?

If a document has not been filed and you have that document with you, a short adjournment should be obtained to enable you to file the document. You should then hand the document to the clerks who sit in front of the associate and wait for the case to be recalled. The case will be heard 'next time around' or 'second time around' which usually means at the end of the morning's list, though it may possibly be heard at the end of that half-hour batch.

(Begin as in (a) above.)

The documents are in order save that the affidavit of service has not been filed. I have that affidavit with me. Would you hear the matter second time around and give leave for the affidavit to be filed?

When the matter is heard second time around, you should remind the registrar of the case, inform them that the affidavit has been filed and ask for the usual compulsory order.

Sir, this matter was stood out to enable the affidavit of service to be filed. This has been done and the rest of the documents are in order. I would ask for the usual compulsory order.

If the defect is serious, you may wish to adjourn the matter to enable the defect to be remedied. In that case, you should ask for an adjournment for a number of days. To complicate matters further, in the Chancery Division, petitions are not in fact adjourned, they are

NOTES:

'stood out', and they are stood out for a number of days rather than weeks or months, though the number of days will usually add up to a precise number of weeks.

(Begin as in (a) above.)

Sir, the petition has not been advertised and the affidavit of service has not been filed. Would you stand the matter out for 28 days to allow for advertisement and to enable service to be effected?

(e) *Settlement*

It may be that the case has settled prior to the hearing and you are instructed not to proceed with the petition. In that case, you should ask for the petition to be dismissed. The agreement should include costs if you are asking the court to make such an order; otherwise, there will be no order as to costs.

Sir, the debtor company has made full payment of the debt, and I would therefore ask you to dismiss the petition with no order as to costs.

If negotiations are afoot, you may wish to obtain an adjournment.

(Begin as in (a) above.)

Sir, the parties are talking and it is hoped that the matter may yet be resolved. In those circumstances, I would ask that the matter be stood out for 28 days.

(f) *Substitution by supporting creditor*

Where the petitioning creditor does not wish to proceed with the application because his debt has been paid or where he or she is dilatory in proceeding with the action, for example, they are seeking a long adjournment, a supporting creditor may apply to be substituted. In the latter situation, the petitioner may oppose the applica-

NOTES:

tion and the registrar will hear submissions from both parties. If the supporting creditor succeeds in his application, he or she will need time to effect the necessary changes in the documents and re-advertise.

Sir, I appear for the supporting creditor ABC Limited, owed the sum of £1,000, and my application is to be substituted today. If you are minded to grant that application, I would ask that the matter be stood out for 28 days to enable re-service and re-advertisement to take place.

(g) *Opposed application*

Where the debtor challenges the validity of the alleged debt, the matter will be referred to a judge for determination of this preliminary point. Where the debtor company opposes the application, for example, on the grounds that it will soon be able to pay off the debt, it may well not have filed any affidavit in opposition. The registrar will often hear the parties' arguments and make an order immediately. If the matter is complex or likely to take some time, the court may stand the petition out to the judge's list.

What if ...?

You miss your petition?

As stated earlier, if your petition is called and you are not in court, the petition will be dismissed. If you have just missed your petition, see one of the clerks of the court (they will be sitting directly in front of the registrar or district judge) and explain what has happened. They will arrange for your matter to be recalled. When this is done, apologise and explain what has happened and ask for the matter to be restored; then proceed in the normal way.

NOTES:

May it please you sir, I appear for the statutory creditor in this matter which I understand was dismissed a few moments ago. Sir, I must apologise for my non-attendance, I was discussing the matter with a representative of the debtor company in the court corridor and did not hear the matter being called. I would ask that the matter be restored and that I be permitted to make my application.

Personal bankruptcy petitions

An individual may be made bankrupt whenever he or she has debts in excess of the 'bankruptcy level', currently £750, the debt is due immediately or at some certain future time, it is unsecured and there is no reasonable prospect of the debtor being able to pay the debt. Again, the debtor will be deemed unable to pay if a statutory demand remains unsatisfied after 3 weeks.

Reference should be made to s 264 of the Act and Part 6 of the Rules.

The procedure is very similar to that for company winding-up petitions and only the significant differences will be noted. Newspaper advertisements of the petition are not required nor is a certificate of compliance. Debtors must be served personally (IR 6.14) at least 14 days before the hearing. The court will usually wish to see a certificate from the creditor or representative that the debt is still owed at the time of the hearing (see *Practice Note* [1987] 1 WLR 120). If the debtor intends to argue that an order should not be made, he or she should file a notice of intention to oppose the petition, seven days before the hearing. However, the fact that one has not been filed does not mean that the application will not be opposed. Hearings are in chambers.

NOTES:

Hearing

Where?	High Court: if the debtor has resided or carried on business in the London insolvency district for the greater part of six months preceding the presentation of the petition, or if the debtor is not resident in England and Wales County court: (if the court has bankruptcy jurisdiction) to the court where the debtor has lived or carried on business in the six months before the issue of the petition
Who?	High Court – bankruptcy registrar District registries and county courts – district judge (Sir/Madam)
Robes?	No

Preliminaries

Bankruptcy petitions are almost always heard in chambers by a registrar or district judge. In the vast majority of cases only the creditor attends.

In the RCJ, you should report to Room TM 1.10 in the Thomas More Building where the clerk will tell you which room number to go to (if you do not know already) and give you a slip to fill in. Go and wait outside. A buzzer will usually sound to tell you when to go in.

In a county court, you should report to the usher who will tell you which district judge you are in front of.

Hearing

The creditor's advocate should introduce the parties and take the court through the paperwork to show that all the procedural steps have been followed and produce the certificate that the debt is still owing. The debtor or advocate should then point to any procedural deficiencies or explain

NOTES:

why the debt is disputed or refer to the notice of intention to oppose. Apart from disputing the debt altogether, the debtor might have offered to compound the debt, in which case the creditor must show that it was reasonable to refuse the offer or the court can dismiss the petition. The debtor might also apply for an interim order with a view to putting together a voluntary arrangement.

Setting aside the statutory demand

In the case of a statutory demand served upon an individual debtor, the method of challenge is set out in IR 6.4: an application should be made in the prescribed form with an affidavit in support within 18 days of service of the demand. Unless the court dismisses the application without further enquiry, the application will be set down for hearing on notice to the creditor. Under IR 6(5)(4), there are four arguments for setting aside a statutory demand:

(a) the debtor has a counterclaim, set off, etc which equals or exceeds the debt;

(b) there are substantial grounds for disputing the debt;

(c) the creditor has security for the debt;

(d) there is some other reason for setting aside the demand.

The first two grounds are by far the most common. The debtor has to satisfy the court that there is a genuine triable issue on any of these points (*Practice Note (Bankruptcy: Statutory Demand: Setting Aside) (No 1/87)* [1987] 1 WLR 119); the test is similar to that on summary judgment, possibly a little less exacting (a statutory demand cannot be set aside conditionally, eg on payment in of a sum of money). If judgment has already been given against the debtor, he or she will only be able to rely on ground (b) – according to the *Practice Note*, the court should not usually allow the

NOTES:

application to be adjourned pending an application to set aside the judgment. In practice, however, the court will often accede to an application provided it is satisfied that the debtor will apply or has applied to set aside the judgment, and certainly if the judgment has been stayed. The debtor can still rely on the counterclaim ground even though the counterclaim could have been raised but was not when the creditor took proceedings in respect of the debt.

The dispute relied on by the debtor must cover the whole of the alleged debt; any undisputed part must be paid off.

Once an application to set aside has been made, the creditor cannot present a bankruptcy petition unless and until the application has been dismissed. If an application is not made within the 18 days allowed, the debtor should apply for an extension of time and if necessary apply for an injunction to restrain a petition (see *Practice Note*). An extension of time can be applied for even after the time limit has expired. An injunction application will be necessary if a petition has been presented. These applications are usually heard in chambers.

The method by which a company can challenge a statutory demand is by applying for an injunction to restrain the presentation of a petition (or advertisement of the petition if one has already been presented). In the High Court, the application is by originating motion and will normally be heard by a judge in open court. In a county court, the application is as for interlocutory injunctions (see Chapter 4 on 'Interlocutory applications'). In either case, the application will be successful if the company can show that there is a genuine dispute in respect of the debt (a prospect of successfully defeating a claim) *and* that the company is solvent, and the petitioning creditor runs a high risk of having to pay

NOTES:

costs on an indemnity basis. Again, the test is probably a little lower than in an application for summary judgment. Again, the company must pay any undisputed element.

Preliminaries

Applications involving individual debtors will usually be heard in chambers but those relating to companies will usually be in open court. In either case, they will follow the form of any other interlocutory application (see Chapter 4). Such applications are particularly analogous to applications for summary judgment. In the case of the individual debtor, the court will have already considered the matter at a paper hearing when it has the option of dismissing the application altogether. If you are for the debtor, therefore, you are in with a fairly good chance. If you are for the company, you must try to argue down the debtor's prospects of success in disputing your claim in a similar way as with summary judgment applications, for example, by showing that the debtor has only recently raised any question of the quality of goods delivered even though they have had them for three years, or that the debtor's evidence is inconsistent, or that he or she relies on a point of law which is not sustainable. If the case involves a company, there will have been no first stage but you should present your arguments along the lines of an application for summary judgment or show that there is a viable counterclaim.

Hearing

The hearing will follow the lines of a normal interlocutory application so you should refer to the Chapter 4, particularly the section on summary judgments.

In either case, the court is likely to award costs on an indemnity basis if the debtor or company is successful.

NOTES:

10 : Licensing

Applications for licences to sell alcohol under the Licensing Act 1964 are superficially fairly straightforward and may seem to some like money for old rope but beware lest you are lulled into a false sense of security. Licensing justices have a great deal of scope to write their own script and the underlying law can get complicated.

There are two main types of licence: on- and off-licences. On-licences cover, for example, restaurants, pubs, clubs and residential hotels. Both types of licence can be restricted as to the type of alcohol that can be sold, eg wine only, beer, cider and wine only, etc. Conditions may be attached to on-licences but not to off-licences; it is quite common for magistrates to ask for assurances or undertakings but these are not strictly enforceable. Licences can also be granted on a provisional basis, which can be particularly useful if a full grant is refused.

Other common applications that you are likely to make are for protection orders, transfers of licences, supper-hour certificates and children's certificates.

In respect of applications for new licences of either main type, magistrates are obliged to consider the following:

(a) whether there is a local need for another licensed premises;

(b) the suitability of the premises;

(c) the suitability of the applicant.

In addition, licensing justices have developed local policies which will contain specific concerns and requirements which must be met. It is extremely important to get hold of

NOTES:

a copy of this. Pay particular attention to the rules on the number of licences which any one applicant may hold, numbers of applicants who may apply for a licence together and the amount of time which it is expected that the applicants or at least one of them will be on the premises.

Need

In practice, the magistrates are rarely too worried about the question of local need in respect of off-licences, particularly in urban areas, but this is not universally the case. On-licences are a different matter. This is one aspect which may be dealt with in the local policy. In addition, the local policy may indicate how the licensing committee wish to have evidence about local need presented. Often, radius maps are required showing the location of the different types of licensed premises in a limited area, usually a quarter or a half mile radius. In some cases, petitions are produced, attempting to show that local customers would use a shop which sold alcohol in a particular location or currently use a shop and it would be convenient if it also sold alcohol. In practice, petitions are rarely helpful and magistrates are often sceptical about them. Expert market research and demographic profiling evidence or evidence from a licensing surveyor will be much more persuasive but it is much more expensive and rarely commissioned until the applicant knows that he or she is likely to face a problem. It can also help to show that the premises will be selling some form of specialist product such as Indian beer which is not generally available in the area.

Premises

At least one copy of the plans for the building must be filed with the application but in practice much more is required.

NOTES:

The fire officer and sometimes the building inspector will visit the premises and make recommendations for alterations as appropriate. The justices themselves will also attend and may give an indication of the way in which they would like the premises to be laid out. Particular concerns are often the security of alcohol when the business is closed, the proximity of the alcohol to any products which might appeal to children, disabled access, compliance with building regulations and so on. Again, the local policy will often have something to say on the matter.

Where the premises need to be adapted to meet the requirements of the court or the local authority, the applicant can apply for a provisional grant. If the applicant's suitability has already been dealt with by the court, they can go ahead with building works with some confidence that a full licence will be granted once the work is satisfactorily completed. Not all courts are prepared to deal with suitability separately, in which case the applicant is running more of a risk. Under a provisional grant, although the applicant can start trading, they may not sell alcohol.

Applicant

The applicant's suitability is often the most important consideration. The applicant(s) will be interviewed by the police and should attend when the magistrates visit the premises. There are certain persons who are disqualified from holding licences altogether and most benches will be concerned about any recent convictions (apart from road traffic offences, unless involving drink-driving!). Applicants are usually expected to be able to speak sufficient English to demonstrate an understanding of the licensing laws (not necessarily easy, even if English is a first language!) and to show that they could deal with any difficult customers. It is

NOTES:

unusual for very young applicants to be successful and experience or training is often a prerequisite. They must also show a relationship to the premises or the company managing the premises.

In the example given below, it is assumed that you are most likely to be representing the applicant(s). The fact that a new business would be in competition with the objector's is not a proper reason for objecting to the application, although it is the most common real life reason for objecting. You must look at the local policy and see whether you have evidence to show, for example, that there is no local need. You can, of course, draw the court's attention to any deficiencies in the premises or the applicant's character, but the court is going to be much more hostile to cross-examination on this.

An extremely useful book to have with you at court is Phillips, J, *Licensing Law Guide*, 1995, Butterworths.

Application

Where? Magistrates' court

Who? Licensing justice (usually between three and five magistrates who are members of the licensing committee)

Robes? No

Preliminaries

The first thing to do is to check that the procedural requirements have all been complied with and that you have copies of all the relevant documents. The list which follows applies to new licence applications – in other cases less is required:

- notices sent to authorities (ie clerk to the justices, police, council, building inspector, fire officer) 21 clear days before the hearing and a certificate of service. There is a

NOTES:

special form which the police ask applicants to complete (Form 687);

- plans for premises;
- radius plan of area;
- advertisements (14 clear days before the hearing);
- petition, if any;
- documents relating to interest in or ownership of the property;
- documents relating to relationship between the applicant and the owner (eg managing agreement with company) including the consent of a co-owner, if any;
- menus, product lists;
- planning permission, if newly developed property.

If the application is for a transfer or protection order, you should also have the written consent of the outgoing licensee.

You must allow plenty of time before the hearing to take the applicant through the standard questions, particularly if there are any doubts about their ability to speak English. First, check what happened at the site visit by the magistrates and whether they seemed worried about anything in particular, and what questions they asked. Check that there was a notice displayed at the premises about the application. The applicant should also have been interviewed by the police; check that this has in fact happened. You should also try to speak to the clerk to the justices who may be able to forewarn you of any problems. Unfortunately, this can be easier said than done in the busier courts, where a huge number of applications are block-listed to start at 10 am. Run through a list of people who are disqualified from holding a licence (and check that the disqualifications do not

NOTES:

apply to the applicant(s). Get a general picture of the layout of the premises, where alcohol will be stored and displayed, what else will be sold there and so on. Find out what the opening hours are, who else is going to be working in the premises, whether they have experience or have had training, and how often the applicant is going to be in attendance.

You also need to check that the applicant understands the main rules about who can be served and who cannot. Unfortunately, many applicants get fixated on 'prostitutes' (not strictly true, the offence is to allow licensed premises to be used as a brothel or allow the premises to be used as the habitual resort or place of meeting of reputed prostitutes; they are perfectly entitled to reasonable refreshment!) and 'policemen in uniform'. A chief concern of magistrates is to prevent the sale of alcohol to those who are under age. They want to know how the licence holder will deal with people whom he suspects to be under age. Find out if your client is participating in the Portman Scheme (voluntary ID cards) or something similar. If not, they will simply have to convince the magistrates that, if someone cannot prove their age, they will refuse to sell them alcohol.

If the court list is particularly long, there may not be enough room in court for everyone who is waiting. You will have to listen out particularly carefully for the number of your case.

The procedure varies quite a lot between courts, or rather between clerks. Some clerks are more 'interventionist' than others and like to ask at least the first few questions. Some Benches want a lot more detail than others, more so at the start of the list than towards the end! Sometimes, they will only want the bare outlines, particularly if a protection order has previously been granted. If you get the chance, try and

NOTES:

watch some of the cases listed before you or ask someone who looks like a regular.

When the case is called, stand up and introduce yourself. The court will ask if there are any objectors. The applicant will come forward to be sworn. Explain what you are applying for. Ask the applicant to state their name and address and then to produce or hand up any documents which have not been filed.

Take the applicant through as many of the following questions as seem appropriate:

> *Can you tell the court what experience you have of selling alcohol to the public?*
> *Where did you work?*
> *How long for?*
> *Did you ever receive any training?*

or:

> *Will you be going on a training course?*

The Bench will not be impressed by empty promises: be sure that your client can be specific about which course, when, how long it lasts, how much it costs and so on. The court may also want to know what will happen to the premises while the applicant is on the course. Whilst training cannot be made a condition of granting a licence, someone who looks as though they are simply saying what the Bench wants to hear will lose all credibility.

> *Have you ever held a licence before?*
> *Have you seen the list of people who are disqualified from holding a licence?*

(If the answer is no, you may be permitted to hand the applicant a copy of a list, in a text book if necessary, showing it to the clerk before you do so.)

NOTES:

Do any of those disqualifications apply to you?
Are you familiar with the licensing laws?
To whom are you not allowed to serve alcohol?
What would you do if you thought someone was under age?
What hours will the shop be open?
Who else will be working there?
When will you be there?
What will happen when you are on holiday?

If there are objectors, they are entitled to cross-examine the applicant.

The magistrates or clerk will then ask any questions and you may need to re-examine to deal with their concerns.

Call any other witnesses on behalf of the applicant.

The court will then seek the views of the police and fire officers who will be sitting in court. Objections are rare, at this stage, but sometimes comments are made.

You are unlikely to need to say much in closing, except perhaps to deal with any particular points that the court has raised. If there is an objector, they will address the court first.

The court will either give its decision straightaway or retire for a short time to consider. If the application is granted, it takes effect straight after the payment of the appropriate court fee – the clerk will usually tell you whether it has been paid or not. If there were objections, the applicant must wait 21 days to allow for any possible appeal. If the application is refused, the applicant can appeal to the Crown Court; the appeal must be issued within 21 days of the hearing.

NOTES:

11 : Appeals and setting aside

If a judgment or other order is made against your client in civil proceedings, there are a number of ways in which he or she can respond. One response, of course, is to give up. However, if a party believes that a mistake has been made, he or she may be able to appeal against the order or apply to have it set aside.

The application will take one of many forms. The choice will depend on the rank of the judicial officer who made the order, the court in which it was made and the type of order that it was.

As a general rule, you should never fight a case in court without knowing what, if any, right of appeal you have if you lose. The unsuccessful client will often immediately want to know what an appeal involves. The thought of a possible appeal may of course be the only source of comfort after the disappointment of losing. Above all, beware of time limits. Decisions on appeals invariably need to be taken promptly. If you think an appeal is on the cards, ask for leave straightaway. This saves your client costs in having to make an extra application. Of course, you may get turned down, but there is a strong chance of refusal in any event.

The Woolf Report recommends a number of reforms to appeals procedures; in particular, that leave to appeal be required for all interlocutory appeals and that leave to appeal should be sought at the end of the hearing, or in writing to the appellate court within three days of the hearing. It is further recommended that all appeals should be of the 'Court of Appeal' type, rather than *de novo* hearings.

NOTES:

You should note that, as a rule, the filing of an appeal does not operate as a stay of execution of the original judgment. A separate application for a stay must be made on notice, in the same way as any other interlocutory application. See RSC Order 58 r 1, Order 59 rr 13 and 19(5), ss 77 and 88 of the County Courts Act 1984, CCR Order 25 r 8 and Order 37 r 8.

Appeals to the Court of Appeal

Civil Division

In general, where the judgment or order was made by a circuit judge or High Court judge, the appeal will be to the Court of Appeal. In certain cases, there is no right of appeal. In many others, no appeal may be made without leave, and leave to appeal should be sought from the trial judge at the time of judgment or on subsequent application. If he refuses, a party can apply to the Court of Appeal for leave and this must be done within four weeks (or earlier period for interlocutory appeals). The rules governing the right of appeal are complex and should be carefully studied. See ss 77–81 of the County Courts Act 1984, the County Court Appeals Order 1991, s 18 Supreme Court Act 1981 and RSC Order 59.

Procedure on appeals to the Court of Appeal is beyond the scope of this work. For details, see RSC Order 59 and the numerous relevant practice directions. Any inexperienced barrister, who is briefed to conduct a full appeal to the Court of Appeal without a leader, should be very sure that they are competent to accept the brief.

Appeals to a High Court judge

An appeal lies to a judge from an interlocutory order made by a master, district judge in the Family Division or district

NOTES:

registrar. Where a master makes a final judgment, having tried the case by consent of the parties, or merely assesses damages, the appeal is to the Court of Appeal.

The application

Where? High Court/district registry – in chambers

Who? High Court judge, or circuit judge/Recorder sitting as a High Court judge

Robes? No

The procedure is governed by RSC Order 58. An appeal lies on questions of both fact and law without leave, except in certain exceptional cases (eg there is no right of appeal from a master's *ex parte* order). A notice of appeal must be issued within five days of the decision which is being appealed (seven days in the case of a district registrar), unless the court directs otherwise.

Preliminaries

The parties will be notified that the appeal is to appear in a 'warned list'. Sometimes (usually outside London), a fixed date is set for hearing. Not later than 48 hours after the notification (or not later than five clear days before the fixed date), the parties must lodge with the court an agreed bundle containing the notice of appeal, the pleadings, copies of all relevant affidavits and exhibits and all relevant orders in the proceedings. The bundle must be paginated and indexed. The parties will not be permitted to rely on any document which is not in the bundle without the leave of the judge. In addition, a chronology and/or skeleton argument should be lodged with the bundle.

The court must be asked to make all original affidavits and exhibits available at the hearing.

NOTES:

Hearing

The appellant opens the appeal, and thereafter it takes the form of a complete re-hearing. It is not formally necessary to re-examine the master's decision and say why it was wrong, but that decision will be given its due weight, and it is sometimes helpful and necessary to do so. You should try to do this as tactfully as possible, even if you think the decision was quite wrong. With the permission of the judge, the parties may rely on affidavits which were not before the master.

Introduce the parties and identify the application:

> *May it please your Lordship, I appear for the appellant, who is the plaintiff in the main action. My learned friend Mrs Aubergine appears for the respondent defendant. This application is by way of appeal from the order of Master Turnip, who granted the defendant unconditional leave to defend on my client's application for summary judgment on 5 April last year. Does your Lordship have the bundle and the affidavits?*

Take the judge to any chronology and/or skeleton argument and ask him if he or she has had time to read it. If so, summarise it very briefly. If not, go through it more carefully. Pay attention to any indication from the judge that they would like you to proceed more quickly, or more slowly, as the case may be.

> *At page 1 of the bundle, your Lordship will find the appellant's skeleton argument. My Lord, the application is argued on two main grounds. Firstly, the fact that the defendant apparently admitted liability in correspondence. Secondly, it is said that the defence put forward does not actually amount to a legal defence, even if the defendant's version of the facts is accepted.*

NOTES:

From here onwards, since the appeal takes the form of a rehearing, argue the case precisely as you would have argued the original application: see Chapter 4 on interlocutory applications. At the end of the hearing, be prepared to deal with the costs of the appeal, and of the 'costs below', ie those of the original hearing before the master/district judge. See also county court 'Final appeals' (below).

Appeals to a county court judge

An appeal lies to a circuit judge from the decision of a district judge as of right (except in small claims cases, or in cases of consent orders). No leave to appeal is required. The appeal may be against findings of fact and/or findings of law.

The procedure depends on whether the district judge's order was made on a final or an interlocutory application. An order is final only if the district judge's decision will finally determine the action *whichever way it is decided*. If this test leaves any room for doubt, reference may be made to RSC Order 59 r 1A which lists which types of application are respectively final or interlocutory for the purpose of appeals to the Court of Appeal.

Interlocutory appeals

The application

Where? County court – in chambers (though the judge may direct that the hearing should be in open court)

Who? Circuit judge or recorder

Robes? No (unless in open court)

The procedure is governed by CCR Order 13 r 1(10) and (11). A notice of appeal should be issued within five days of the

NOTES:

date of the order complained of. There is no need to specify grounds of appeal.

Preliminaries

The notice must be served on the other side at least two days before the hearing. Check that the matter is indeed 'interlocutory'. This is regularly the subject of argument. It is nearly always to the advantage of one side to argue that the appeal should take the form of submissions, rather than a full rehearing. Unless you are certain on this point, be prepared to deal with the matter as if it were a 'final' appeal, in case the judge takes this view of it. Otherwise, prepare for the hearing as for any other interlocutory hearing.

Hearing

The appeal takes the form of a rehearing. The appellant opens the hearing (even if he would not have opened the original hearing of the application):

> *May it please your Honour, I appear for the appellant, who is the plaintiff in the main action. My learned friend Mr Marrow appears for the respondent defendant. This application is by way of appeal from the order of District Judge Swede, who granted the defendant unconditional leave to defend on my client's application for summary judgment on 5 April this year. As your Honour is aware, this being an interlocutory matter, the appeal is of course by way of rehearing. Has your Honour had a chance to look through the papers?*

Depending on the reply to that last question, introduce the case in more or less detail. Then proceed with the rehearing, precisely as you would have argued the original application: see Chapter 4. At the end of the hearing, be prepared to deal with the costs of the appeal, and of the 'costs below' ie, those

NOTES:

of the original hearing before the district judge. See also 'Final appeals' (below).

Final appeals

Where? County court – in open court

Who? Circuit judge or recorder

Robes? Yes

The procedure in these cases is governed by CCR Order 37 r 6. A notice of appeal must be issued and served on the other side within 14 days of the date of the decision complained of. The notice must state the grounds of appeal.

The judge may, on such terms as they think fit, set aside or vary the original order, substitute any other order for it, remit the matter for rehearing by the same or another district judge, or order a new trial before a circuit judge.

The appellant must show grounds for interfering with the decision of the district judge. Judges must exercise their appellate discretion judicially and make an order only for good and sufficient reason. If the appeal is against an exercise of discretion by the district judge, the appeal will only be allowed on the ground that no reasonable district judge could have exercised their discretion in the way complained of. Findings of fact may be overturned, but in practice this will happen only if the appellant can show that the evidence was simply not sufficient to support the findings of fact which the district judge made.

Preliminaries

It is advisable for the appellant to prepare a bundle, to be agreed if possible. This should contain the pleadings, any documentary evidence adduced at trial or expert reports,

NOTES:

the order of the district judge, a note of the judgment and a copy of the notice of appeal.

As to the note of the judgment, if the proceedings were recorded or transcribed, the court will provide a copy of the transcript on payment of a fee. Otherwise, it is open to either party to request a copy of the district judge's note of the judgment and/or signed notes of the evidence. If no other note is available, the parties may rely on the notes taken by the advocates at the original hearing. If possible, these should be agreed between the two sides, and the note should be sent to the district judge well in advance of the appeal for any comments. See also s 80 of the County Courts Act 1984.

It is also advisable to prepare a skeleton argument in complex cases.

Hearing

In this chapter, we take as example a typical civil case where a plumber has been unsuccessfully sued by a dissatisfied customer. The customer appeals on the basis that findings of fact were not supported by the evidence and that a point of law was wrongly decided.

The appellant opens the hearing:

> *May it please your Honour, I appear for the appellant, who was the plaintiff in the original action. My learned friend Miss Parsnip appears for the respondent defendant. This is my client's appeal from the order of District Judge Carrot, who dismissed her claim for damages for breach of contract. The trial took place on 5 April this year. Has your Honour had a chance to look through the papers?*

Once again, the answer to this question will dictate the pace at which you proceed. If the answer is no, you might continue:

Notes:

May I take your Honour to the pleadings. From the particulars of claim, your Honour will see that my client engaged the services of the defendant, who is a plumber, to attend to the installation of bathrooms in her new home. Paragraphs 4 and 5 state that the work was carried out, and that the plaintiff paid £1,250 plus VAT. At paragraph 6, your Honour will see that my client became dissatisfied with the quality of the work, and there is a list of the problems which became apparent.

Go on to state what defence was put forward and briefly summarise the evidence which was adduced at trial including any expert reports, etc subject of course to indications from the judge as to what he would or would not like to hear about.

Meanwhile, if the judge indicated at the outset that they have read the papers, simply give the briefest possible summary of the case:

Your Honour is therefore aware that the plaintiff's claim was based on unsatisfactory workmanship which she alleged against the defendant and which became apparent after she had paid for the work.

Once you have dealt with the outline of the case, move on to the decision of the district judge:

At page 28 of the bundle, your Honour will see the note of judgment of the learned District Judge.

If the judge has indicated that they have not already looked through the papers, take them through the district judge's judgment, again paying heed to any hints as to how quickly you should go. If the judge has already read the judgment, omit this paragraph:

The judgment begins with a review of the evidence.

NOTES:

(Give a concise summary of the evidence as dealt with by the district judge.)

> *After reviewing the evidence, at the top of page 3 the learned District Judge makes certain findings of fact. He finds, firstly, that the work was completed on 10 March 1993, secondly, that the plaintiff made a full inspection of the work later that day, and thirdly, that on 11 March the plaintiff signed a certificate to the effect that she was satisfied with the work which the defendant had carried out. Then, at page 4, the learned District Judge addresses himself to the law, and holds that the plaintiff was bound by the certificate which she signed and that she was not entitled to complain subsequently about the defects.*

Then move to the notice of appeal:

> *The plaintiff's notice of appeal is at page 33 of the bundle. The grounds of appeal are, firstly, that the evidence did not support the learned District Judge's finding that the plaintiff fully inspected the work, and, secondly, that the District Judge erred as a matter of law in holding that the certificate bound the plaintiff and prevented her from complaining later. The plaintiff, therefore, appeals against the dismissal of her claim and against the order that she pay the defendant's costs.*

Now it is time to develop your arguments in support of the appeal. Your argument should be clearly divided into distinct points. For clarity, it is often helpful to number these. The points you make should be expressly linked to the numbered grounds given in your notice of appeal:

> *Your Honour, as to the first ground, the District Judge found as a fact that the plaintiff fully inspected the work in question. This finding could only have been based on two matters, namely the certificate which the*

NOTES:

plaintiff signed, which said that she was satisfied with the work, and secondly, the oral testimony of the defendant, who said that the plaintiff inspected the new pipework both inside and out before signing the certificate. In my submission, the evidence did not support that finding. Firstly, may I refer to the wording on the certificate itself, a copy of which is at page 34 of the bundle ...

And so on. Conclude, as ever, with a formula such as:

The plaintiff appeals on those grounds, and seeks either a judgment in her favour, or an order that the matter be reheard by another District Judge. Unless your Honour would like to hear from me on any other point, those are my submissions for the appellant.

The judge will then call upon the respondent's advocate, who will put the arguments in his client's favour in exactly the same way.

The judge will make a decision, usually there and then, though the judgment may be reserved. He or she will then invite the parties to deal with costs (see Chapter 12).

Costs, as always, tend to follow the event, ie the party succeeding on appeal is normally entitled to his costs of the appeal. An order may also be made in respect of the 'costs below', ie the costs of the original hearing by district judge. If the appeal results in a judgment in favour of the appellant, 'costs below' will normally be awarded to them. If the order on appeal is for a rehearing, the judge may reserve the issue of any part of the costs to the rehearing, to be determined once the overall rights and wrongs of the case have been re-decided. There are cases where a successful appellant does not recover his costs of the first hearing, eg where he or she wins by adducing evidence at a rehearing which they might have adduced at the first hearing.

NOTES:

Setting aside judgment

Setting aside provides a remedy where a party claims that a miscarriage of justice has occurred by reason of something other than an error by the trial judge. Where the latter is alleged, the appropriate course is to appeal.

In a county court, CCR Order 37 r 1 provides a general power for the judge on application to order a rehearing, where no error of the court is alleged. This power may be exercised where, for example, one side succeeded by means of a fraudulent trick, where fresh evidence has emerged which could not have been made available for the first hearing, where a witness is exposed as a perjurer, or in general where it can be shown that a miscarriage of justice may well have occurred.

CCR Order 37 r 2 (RSC Order 35 r 2) empowers the court to set aside any judgment or order obtained against a party in his absence.

By CCR Order 37 r 3 (RSC Order 13 r 7(5)), the court has the power to set aside judgment where it appears that the summons or other originating process was posted to the defendant but never received.

CCR Order 37 r 4 (RSC Order 13 r 9 and cf Order 19 r 9) provides that judgment entered in default of a defence being delivered can be set aside, varied or confirmed.

Some common principles govern these powers. Firstly, it is usually necessary for the applicant to show the possibility of a miscarriage of justice if the judgment is not set aside. This is done by demonstrating that there is a triable issue of fact or law, as for an application for summary judgment (see Chapter 4).

NOTES:

Secondly, even if the 'triable issue' test is not satisfied, the court will usually set aside judgment if the proceedings were technically flawed. This is the basis for setting aside on failure of postal service, and the same principle applies in cases of defendants' non-attendance or default judgment: if the plaintiff was not technically entitled to enter judgment, it will be set aside.

Thirdly, the conduct of the parties is taken into account. If judgment was entered because a party failed to appear at trial or to deliver a defence, that party should explain the reason for their default. If there is no reasonable excuse, the usual result will be that judgment is set aside, but the defaulting party is ordered to pay all the costs up to the time of setting aside. In extreme cases, however, the court may in its discretion refuse to set aside judgment.

Overall, the court will look at the prejudice which either party might suffer as a result of the grant or refusal of the application to set aside.

Applications to set aside are made and heard in exactly the same way as any other interlocutory application: see Chapter 4.

What if ...?

You are instructed just before the hearing, and you realise there are no grounds of appeal?

It can happen that an excess of enthusiasm leads to an appeal being made although it has no chance of success. If you find yourself at court on such an occasion, you should carefully consider what to do. Of course, it is possible to proceed and 'go through the motions'. However, appellate courts rightly discourage litigants from pursuing hopeless appeals, and will not show you any indulgence. Your client

NOTES:

may be penalised by an award of indemnity costs or, in an extreme case, costs could be awarded against the party's advisers. You should consider withdrawing at the door of the court. Obviously, you would have to explain to the client why it was inadvisable to go on, and apologise for the situation having arisen. In this situation, it might yet be possible achieve something by negotiation: for example, if you offer to withdraw your appeal, the other side might accept terms proposed by you in respect of the execution of the judgment.

On appeal, your opponent raises a point or calls evidence which should have been taken at the original hearing?

This is permissible in an appeal by way of rehearing, but not in an appeal from a 'final' order by way of submissions. If this rule is being broken, object immediately:

> *I am very sorry to interrupt, but my learned friend is not entitled to adduce new evidence on this point. These matters were known about at the time of the hearing, but no evidence was called to support the point.*

Do not simply rely on the judge to object for you. If the judge fails to intervene and makes a wrong decision as a result, your remedies by way of further appeal will be much more complicated and expensive.

NOTES:

12 : Costs and legal aid

One of the Woolf Report's major criticisms of litigation, particularly in the county court, is that costs are disproportionate to the value of the claim, and all too often exceed the value of the claim. Indeed, this has been a theme of many previous reports, not least the Civil Justice Review in its report in 1988 (*Civil Justice Review: Report of the Review Body on Civil Justice*, Cm 394, HMSO, 1988). This concern underpins most of the report's recommendations and the first draft rule requires the court to deal with a case in a way which is proportionate to the amount involved, the importance or complexity of the issues and the parties' financial positions.

The Woolf Report proposes a number of major changes to the costs provisions, particularly in respect of 'fast-track' cases where a fixed costs regime is proposed, and it is anticipated that only the advocate will attend the hearing. Legal professional bodies are expected to encourage their members to undertake litigation on a fixed fee basis in other cases, either for the whole case, or for stages of it. It is also recommended that courts should take into account to a greater degree than they do at present the manner in which the successful party has conducted the proceedings and the outcome of individual issues. Other recommendations include: power to order payment of interim costs, a new standard basis of taxation ('reasonable to both parties'), power to order the financially stronger party to pay the costs of a particular procedure, whatever the outcome, power to deal with costs after a settlement and changes to the rules to reflect more precisely the obligations the new rules will place on parties.

NOTES:

Even without the implications of the above, the advocate should always be aware of the impact of costs at all stages of litigation. The clear intention is that lawyers or clients who waste costs will be made to pay.

Summary

Firstly, in most cases, costs will 'follow the event', ie the person who loses pays the person who wins. Secondly, the court has a discretion to make a different arrangement as to who to pay the costs, and this is likely to become more common post-Woolf. Thirdly, in some cases, the rules provide for a different 'default position'.

The usual orders

There are a number of different orders which the court can make, which are set out in RSC Order 62 r 3(6), which is reproduced in the *Green Book* section on 'Costs and Fees'. They are summarised below. For the purpose of convenience, it is assumed that the orders are made in favour of a plaintiff.

Costs or *costs in any event*	The defendant pays the plaintiff's costs, whether or not the plaintiff is ultimately successful. If this order is made at a final hearing, the plaintiff is entitled to have his or her costs taxed straightaway.
Costs reserved	If the plaintiff wins at the end of the day, the defendant will have to pay the plaintiff's costs, unless the court makes a different decision at the time. This rule does not apply in family cases, where, if costs are reserved, the applicant will not get any costs at all unless you remember

NOTES:

to ask the court to make a specific order for costs.

Costs here and below — If the plaintiff has succeeded in an appeal, the defendant will have to pay both the costs involved in the appeal hearing and the costs of the proceedings in the lower court.

Costs in the cause/ in the application — If the plaintiff is awarded costs at the final hearing, the defendant will have to pay these costs as well but, if the defendant gets costs at the final hearing, the plaintiff will have to pay.

Plaintiff's costs in the cause — If judgment is given in the plaintiff's favour at the final hearing, the defendant will have to pay these costs. If the plaintiff loses, however, he or she will not have to pay the defendant's costs.

Costs thrown away — The defendant will have to pay the plaintiff any costs which have been wasted as a result of a hearing being ineffective or where it is later set aside.

The court might also make an order for 'costs in the usual terms': this means that there is some specific 'default' position set out in the rules which is to be followed. The court can also make 'no order for costs' in which case each side will have to pay their own costs. If nothing is said on the face of the order this also means 'no order'.

There is an extensive commentary in both the *Green Book* and *White Book* as to the practice of the courts when it comes to costs. Other useful materials to consult include Cook, MJ, *Cook on Costs*, 2nd edn, 1995, Butterworths; Hansen, O, *Legal Aid in Practice*, 3rd edn, 1993, Legal Action Group and the

NOTES:

Legal Aid Handbook, which is published annually by Sweet & Maxwell.

There is insufficient space in this book to deal with costs in huge detail, but we will deal with some of the main points you are likely to encounter, concentrating in the main on county court costs. See Order 38 of the County Court Rules.

Cases where an order for costs is deemed to have been made

(a) when a summons to set aside judgment is dismissed (the applicant has to pay the costs);

(b) when a party applies to discontinue an action (the applicant has to pay the costs);

(c) when a party accepts a payment into court by notice in writing (the party who made the payment has to pay costs up to the date of the notice).

However, the court has a discretion in unusual circumstances to make a different costs order.

Common cases where costs do not follow the event

(a) when the pleadings are amended (the party making the amendment has to pay the costs thrown away);

(b) costs of an application to extend a time limit (the party making the application has to pay).

Again, the court still has a discretion in unusual circumstances to make a different costs order.

Common examples of cases in which the court will exercise its discretion against the successful party

(a) when a party refuses a 'Calderbank' offer and fails to better it;

(b) when a party asks for discovery before action, he will

NOTES:

usually have to pay the costs of that application in any event;

(c) where a party has deliberately exaggerated the value of the claim (for example, by saying that it is worth more than £3,000, in order to take it out of the small claims jurisdiction. This often happens where a loss of use claim is made in a road traffic accident case but not quantified);

(d) when a case is brought in the High Court which should have been started in the county court;

(e) where a party is successful but has 'brought the proceedings on themselves' by their conduct, eg by misleading the other side;

(f) where a party has rushed to litigation without a letter before action.

Summary judgment

See Chapter 4.

Both parties are partly successful

It is important to ask the court to deal with the apportionment of costs at the hearing. The court can either apportion the costs on the basis of 'separate issues', if it is truly possible to split the issues and the attendant costs up. However, the preferred approach is to divide the costs up on a proportionate basis: see *Cinema Press Ltd v Pictures and Pleasures Ltd* [1945] 1 All ER 440.

Counterclaims

Be careful that the court makes an order which deals with the counterclaim specifically: an order which does not will not include these costs. If judgment is given on both the claim and counterclaim, the court will tax the costs of the claim first and then identify the additional costs which have

NOTES:

been incurred by the counterclaim. This will most often favour the plaintiff. The same will apply if both claim and counterclaim are dismissed. If you want the court to do something different, you must remember to ask for a specific order at the end of the hearing. The court retains its absolute discretion: see CCR Order 21 r 4(4) and RSC Order 15 r 2(4).

Multiple parties

Provided it was reasonable for a plaintiff to involve more than one defendant in the proceedings, he or she will usually be entitled to recover costs from the unsuccessful defendant, from which the successful defendant's costs will have to be paid. This is known as a *Bullock* order. In the same circumstances, if such a plaintiff is legally aided or insolvent, a *Sanderson* order can be made under which the unsuccessful defendant pays the successful defendant directly. If the defendants are found jointly liable, the court will usually apportion the costs on the same basis as the liability. If the plaintiff loses the case altogether, he or she will have to pay the costs of all the other parties.

Assessed costs

Costs must be assessed by the court where costs are payable on the lower scale or in scale 1 cases, where the solicitor for the party with the benefit of a costs order asks the court to assess them (rather than submit them for taxation). There is a ceiling on the costs which may be awarded (see Appendix C to CCR Order 38). In Scale 2 cases, the court has a discretion to assess the costs without limit. In practice, the court will often assess costs where it is blatantly obvious that the costs which are sought are much less than those that might be awarded on taxation; this is particularly common in possession cases. The advantage is that the costs are ascertained there and then without the need to draw up a

NOTES:

bill, etc. In practice, most courts have a going rate, but they may want to know what costs have been incurred, and to see counsel's brief, so it is particularly important that the brief is marked if you think you are likely to want costs to be assessed.

County court scales

There are at present three county court scales linked to the amount of money recovered by the successful party: the lower scale (£25–£100); Scale 1 (£100–£3,000) and Scale 2 (over £3,000). The court still has an absolute discretion on what costs to award, but it is far less likely to move up or down the scales when the action is for the recovery of a sum of money only, unless, for example, the case has involved a difficult point of law, or unusually complex facts (cf, the typical arguments for taking a case out of the small claims jurisdiction).

Cases remitted from the High Court to a county court

The costs incurred before the case was transferred down *may* be allowed on the High Court scale, up to the date of transfer, whatever the amount finally recovered. However, this is less likely to happen if the case should not have been in the High Court in the first place and the usual rule is that the scale will depend on the amount outstanding at the time of transfer to the county court if that is less than the sum claimed.

When is an order for legal aid taxation needed?

Under regulation 107 of the Civil Legal Aid (Remuneration) Regulations 1989, an order for taxation must be obtained before payment can be made (unless principally, the legal aid certificate has been discharged, for example, at the end of the proceedings or the costs are under £1,000 including

NOTES:

counsel's fees but not VAT, or it was a family case in the magistrates' court). Orders for legal aid taxation are frequently asked for and granted at interlocutory hearings, but this should not necessarily happen, particularly where the order made is for 'costs reserved' or 'costs in the cause', and especially in family cases. If it seems likely that the interlocutory hearing will effectively put an end to the matter (as is often the case in applications for injunctions), the court is likely to be receptive to an application for legal aid taxation, but the chances are it will be making no order for costs as well.

The legally aided party

The fact that one party has the benefit of legal aid, whether successful or unsuccessful, should not affect the exercise of the court's discretion in making a costs' order. Strictly speaking, what the court should do before making any order is to consider what is reasonable for the legally aided party to pay having regard to all the circumstances, including the party's financial resources (s 17 Legal Aid Act 1988). If the party has no means with which to meet a costs' order, no order should be made. If the court does not know anything about the party's financial circumstances, the question of costs ought to be adjourned for proper determination and the court should conduct a means enquiry with evidence by affidavit or orally. The court may not take into account the party's home or the tools and implements of his trade. You should not, therefore, assume that because a party is legally aided there is no prospect of enforcing an order for costs.

In practice, what the court often does is to make an order for costs 'not to be enforced without leave', leaving the door permanently open for the other side to enforce the costs order if the legally aided party's financial position should change.

NOTES:

It should also be remembered that the court can make an order that the costs of the unassisted party be set off against any costs or damages he may be ordered to pay the assisted party (*Lockley v National Blood Transfusion Service* [1992] 2 All ER 589).

The non-legally aided party

Apart from the above considerations, where one party is legally aided and the other party is not, there is provision for costs to be recovered from the Legal Aid Board (s 18 Legal Aid Act) where the non-legally aided party is successful, the court would have made an order against the other side but for the considerations under s 17 of that Act and the court is satisfied that the non-legally aided party will suffer severe financial hardship unless the order is made. Such an order cannot, however, be made straightaway at the end of the hearing; the court must notify the Legal Aid Board. An application under s 18 may be made at any time and in any manner in which an order for costs might normally be sought.

Certificates and special allowances

CCR Order 38 r 9 allows the court, at the hearing or at taxation, to award an amount in excess of that which would normally be allowed in a county court. This provision may be used, for example, where a solicitor-advocate has appeared against counsel in a case which is certified fit for counsel. It is in practice not commonly used, but worth thinking about when the hourly rates which would be allowed to a solicitor would not sufficiently reflect the effort involved in preparing and presenting the case. The Legal Aid in Civil Proceedings (Remuneration) Regulations 1994 (regulation 5) also allow the area authority to allow more than any prescribed rates.

NOTES:

Certificates for counsel

A cause of some confusion. Certificates are required in any interlocutory matter in the High Court. CCR Order 38 r 8 provides that in an interlocutory application in a county court counsel can be paid what a solicitor would have been paid for hearing unless the judge or district judge certifies that it was proper for counsel to attend. The same applies in an action for the recovery of money only when there is no defence and the defendant does not attend at the hearing. The confusion arises when hearings are listed as final hearings, but one party makes an application to adjourn, etc such that the order made is an interlocutory order. There is also considerable confusion about whether certificates are required in all legally aided matters or not and in any hearings conducted in chambers. If in doubt, ask for a certificate. The judge will usually either tell you that you do not need one or give you a certificate just to be on the safe side.

Legal aid statutory charge

We do not propose to go into great detail about the effect of the statutory charge in this book. In summary, in all cases where a party preserves or recovers money or property which has been the subject matter of a dispute, he or she will be expected to pay his or her own legal costs. This applies even if the case is settled without actually going to court. There are some exceptions to the rule, for example, the first £2,500 recovered is exempt in most family cases. In general terms, civil legal aid should be seen as a loan in any case where a party is likely to get an order for money or property. It is important to make sure your client knows about the charge and that you understand it properly yourself so that you can make sure that, eg property is not argued about when it need not be. It is particularly important in ancillary relief cases: you should not put a property or part-share in issue if you do not dispute entitlement to it. See Chapter 5,

NOTES:

but if the property recovered or preserved is to be used as a home or to purchase a home, a certificate pursuant to Regulation 96 should be obtained so that the statutory charge will be deferred.

Misbehaviour by lawyers

The court has extensive powers to ensure that if lawyers make mistakes their clients and the other parties do not have to pay for them, and you are not necessarily safe just because the judge does not say anything at the hearing. The district judge can deal with wasted costs at the taxation stage. A lawyer will have to pay costs personally if they have been incurred improperly, unreasonably or negligently, or where they have been wasted by a failure to conduct the proceedings with reasonable competence and expedition. However, a high standard of proof is required and it must be shown that the lawyer's default did in fact cause costs to be wasted. Further, the application, which the court should be very slow to initiate, should not be made until after the hearing. It is up to the court what procedure to adopt (and a consideration will be the amount of costs in issue), but it is extremely unlikely that you would be called to account without any warning, and you must be given the opportunity to 'defend' yourself.

What if ...?

At court you discover that there has been a change in your legally aided client's financial circumstances?

If the client is legally aided, you must advise them that it will affect their entitlement to legal aid and that both of you have a duty to report this to the Legal Aid Board. If you are counsel, you should notify the solicitor after the hearing so that it can be dealt with.

NOTES:

You forget to ask for a certificate for counsel?

The slip rule can be used if a judge does not make an order which he was not asked to make, but would have done if he had been asked: see *Re Earl Inchcape* [1942] 2 All ER 157. If you are likely to go back to court again on another occasion, you can ask the court for the certificate then, or you could write to the court. You can also ask for the matter to be raised at the taxation stage: the district judge has power to grant a certificate under CCR Order 38 r 21(4). Otherwise, you will be paid as if the case had been conducted by a solicitor.

You think your own side may be in danger of a wasted costs order?

A situation which calls for the utmost tact. You need to try to establish, if possible, whether the fault lies with the lawyer or with the lay client and you should always try to discuss it in private with the lawyer first. If it is the lawyer's fault, they may be prepared to indicate that the client will not be expected to pay the costs which have been wasted. If it is the client's fault, you will have the thankless task of warning them what to expect. In such situations, if there is any conflict between the lawyer and the client, it will be necessary to advise the client of the fact and say that they should discuss it between themselves but that if it cannot be resolved informally they may need to take independent advice. In cases like this, seek the advice of a more senior colleague. If it comes up in the court room and you were not expecting it, the best policy is not to speculate but to ask for an adjournment so that you can take proper instructions and examine the relevant file. If, however, you do know the full background, you must not mislead the court simply in order to save the face of your professional client, overwhelming as that temptation might be. If it is your own fault, or you think

NOTES:

that it might be, ask for an adjournment so that you can prepare yourself properly and talk it through with a colleague.

NOTES:

Index